Relationship Magic

About the Author

Guy Finley is a bestselling self-help writer and internationally renowned spiritual teacher. He is the author of over forty-five books and audio/video programs, including his acclaimed seminal book *The Secret of Letting Go*. His popular books and audio programs, several of which have become international bestsellers, have sold over two million copies worldwide.

Considered a modern-day mystic and practical philosopher, Guy's wisdom cuts straight to the heart of today's most pressing personal and social issues—relationships, success, addiction, stress, peace, happiness, freedom—and leads the way to a higher life.

He has presented over five thousand unique self-realization seminars to thousands of grateful students throughout North America and Europe over the past thirty-five years. Each week over one hundred thousand subscribers in 142 countries read his inspiring Key Lesson Newsletter.

Published in more than twenty-six languages, his popular works are widely endorsed by doctors, business professionals, and religious leaders of all denominations. Among many others, his popular titles include: *The Secret of Your Immortal Self; The Secret of Letting Go; The Seeker, The Search, The Sacred; The Courage to Be Free; The Essential Laws of Fearless Living; Let Go and Live in the Now; Freedom From the Ties That Bind*; and *Design Your Destiny*.

Guy has been a featured guest on over seven hundred television and radio shows, including national appearances on ABC, NBC, CBS, CNN, and NPR. He is a regular contributor to the Huffington Post, Beliefnet, Positively Positive, and many more.

As the founding director of Life of Learning Foundation (a nonprofit center for self-study in Merlin, Oregon), he presents four self-realization classes weekly. These meetings are ongoing and open to the public. He also hosts online courses through Life of Learning's Wisdom School. In 2011, he launched the OneJourney Project, OneJourney.net, an award-winning interfaith website illuminating the unseen spiritual unity underlying all world religions.

Guy Finley

Relationship Magic
Waking Up Together

Llewellyn Publications
Woodbury, Minnesota

FIRST EDITION
First Printing, 2018

Cover design by Kristi Carlson

Llewellyn Publications is a registered trademark of Llewellyn Worldwide Ltd.

Library of Congress Cataloging-in-Publication Data
Names: Finley, Guy, author.
  Title: Relationship magic : waking up together / Guy Finley.
  Description: First edition. | Woodbury, Minnesota : Llewellyn Publications, [2018].
  Identifiers: LCCN 2018024775 (print) | LCCN 2018037137 (ebook) | ISBN 9780738755687 (ebook) | ISBN 9780738754093 (alk. paper)
  Subjects: LCSH: Love. | Interpersonal relations.
  Classification: LCC BF575.L8 (ebook) | LCC BF575.L8 .F525 2018 (print) | DDC 158.2—dc23
  LC record available at https://lccn.loc.gov/2018024775

Llewellyn Worldwide Ltd. does not participate in, endorse, or have any authority or responsibility concerning private business transactions between our authors and the public.

All mail addressed to the author is forwarded, but the publisher cannot, unless specifically instructed by the author, give out an address or phone number.

Any Internet references contained in this work are current at publication time, but the publisher cannot guarantee that a specific location will continue to be maintained. Please refer to the publisher's website for links to authors' websites and other sources.

Llewellyn Publications
A Division of Llewellyn Worldwide Ltd.
2143 Wooddale Drive
Woodbury, MN 55125-2989
www.llewellyn.com

Printed in the United States of America

Other Books by Guy Finley

The Secret of Your Immortal Self
The Secret of Letting Go
The Seeker, The Search, The Sacred
The Courage to Be Free
The Essential Laws of Fearless Living
Let Go and Live in the Now
Freedom From the Ties That Bind
Design Your Destiny

Audio Albums

Secrets of Spiritual Success
The Six Characteristics of Higher Self-Command
Seven Steps to Oneness
The Meditative Life
Secrets of Being Unstoppable
Being Fearless and Free
The Meaning of Life
Forever Free

DVD Albums

Life Is Real Only When You Are
Wisdom's Path to the Happiness Within

For a complete list of over 300 works by Guy Finley, visit www.guyfinley.org. You can also sign up right on the home page to receive an inspiring free Key Lesson each week by email.

Dedication

Trying to thank, by name, all the good people who had a hand in helping make this book a reality would be like a tree hoping to recall all the sunlight and breezes that ever touched and brushed its leaves—nourishing it, moving it, challenging and strengthening it over its many years on this earth.

So, my thanks to *all* of you, and to all—including those who set themselves against me—a measure of whatever love is mine to offer.

To VH: without whom the ideas in this book may have never come into the light.

To Dr. Ellen Dickstein: a special tip of the hat for your dedicated efforts and fine skills in helping to make this a better book for all who will turn its pages.

But...most of all, to my wife, Patricia: thank you.

Side by side—and now for almost four decades—she has walked with me through "thick and thin"—helping me more than anyone else on this earth to understand just how deep, ceaseless, and true runs the Magic of Love.

She is, and always will be, my closest friend, "chief editor," and consummate lover.

—GF

Contents

Foreword

By Dr. Laura Markham

It's common wisdom that relationships are hard. They may begin with the magic of romance, but as we start to weave our lives together, tensions inevitably surface. Differing needs, wants, and perspectives are part of every human relationship, and most of us don't learn how to work through conflict constructively while we're growing up.

Most relationship books reassure us that fights are essential to work out our differences, as long as couples "fight fair." But in *Relationship Magic: Waking Up Together*, Guy Finley issues a radical challenge to the assumption that fights with our partners can be healthy. After all, what does a fair fight look like when each person is sure they're right? We think we're defending something important, so we lash out; we use our knowledge of our partner's tender places to wound; we insist that our partner concede that we're right and they're wrong. Somehow, we think that holding our partner responsible for our pain will stop it from hurting. Too often, even when we try to "fight fair," our fights leave a trail of wreckage. And because most fights end in stalemates that don't resolve anything, the same conflicts simmer and erupt repeatedly, solidifying into barriers that create a growing distance between us.

Many couples try to avoid destructive fighting, but the alternative is usually storing up unexpressed grievances. Unfortunately, research confirms the wisdom many couples learn from painful experience: this strategy leads to resentment and contempt, which inevitably erode love.

It's not surprising that most couples feel trapped between these two damaging paths—fighting or stuffing our needs—neither of which leads to the relationship we know in our hearts is possible. But what if there were another answer? What if you could avoid damaging fights altogether, but instead of accumulating resentments, you could use those challenging moments to grow? What if you could turn any heated exchange into a healing turning point?

That's the Relationship Magic prescribed by Guy Finley in this book. Drawing on his many years as a spiritual teacher, Finley applies the timeless guidance of spiritual growth to building intimate relationships, reframing our perspective on what's actually happening when we fight and showing us how to dissolve resentments to create the relationship we long for.

We often believe that our relationship clashes are caused by our partner's failings, even if we don't say that aloud. In our fairer moments, we blame conflicting needs and wants. But Finley shows us how our relationship struggles are an expression of the pain we each carry and bring into our relationships. That pain can't be healed by visiting it on each other. It *can* be healed by the power of love.

In this book, Guy Finley gives you the tools to dissolve the pain causing distance between you and your partner and to strengthen your connection with everyone you love. You'll learn how to use the power of love to heal recurring conflicts. You'll learn how to stop any fight before it starts.

This book will also show you how to renew your relationship, clearing away the stagnant resentments and rekindling your passion. Couples often complain that they just don't "feel the love in the same way anymore." Finley points out that for love to flourish, it must be constantly renewed, and shows us how to do that. Love isn't a feeling we either have or don't have. Love is a choice we make minute by minute.

The magic in this book is learning how to let love be your answer. Just as love for their children gives parents the motivation to heal their ability to love unconditionally, romantic partnerships give us the opportunity and the incentive to dissolve the old patterns that limit us. By showing us our hidden triggers, supporting us to bring our conscious awareness to the pain we carry, and blessing us with the grace of healing, our love for our partner becomes the catalyst for our own growth.

At core, every choice we make is between love and fear. In this book, Guy Finley shows us how to choose love even in those moments of pain and drama, use the power of love to become better human beings, and create the relationship we long for.

Introduction
What This Book Is All About

There is a timeless teaching about love and relationships whose simple beauty conveys an undying wisdom. Its words are encouraging and full of hope at the same time, singing of possibilities that few of us have ever dared dream. And yet none of these promises are directly spoken; rather, they are hidden in an old Zen saying that I've paraphrased here as best I'm able to recollect:

> *Birds fly through the open skies, but no matter how many times they take wing, there is no end to those skies through which they fly.*
>
> *Fish swim in water, and yet no matter how great the distance they swim, there is no end to the water through which they swim.*[1]

---

1. Kazuaki Tanahasi, ed., *Moon in a Dewdrop: Writings of Zen Master Dogen*, reissue ed. (New York: North Point Press, 1995).

This elegant illustration speaks to us of a boundless relationship between bird and sky, between fish and water. Assuming we can feel something of the beauty in this timeless correlation, we come to the first part of a single great secret that lies at the heart of relationship magic.

Just as bird and sky, fish and water are made for one another, inextricably involved in an endless affair... *so is there a limitless relationship between love... and us*. Only in this instance, relationships are our skies, our waters. We are made for one another.

A Single Insight That Answers Your Pressing Relationship Questions

It often feels as if our relationships—especially as they mature—give rise to more questions than they seemed to answer when we first became involved with our partner. The following four questions show us that we're not alone in our concerns, as well as setting the stage for us to look into a single insight that holds the answer to all of them at the same time.

1. Why is it that even though I have a loving partner, there are times when I still feel so empty, as if I'm alone?

2. Things couldn't have been better when we first started out, but that sparkle is starting to fizzle! Where did the love go?

3. When we first got together we'd talk for hours on end, but now we hardly talk at all. It's as if we have nothing to share anymore... besides our practical affairs. What's happened to us?

4. We're trying to spice up our relationship with little to no success. I know we love each other, but the only time things seem to get "hot" is when we're in a fight of some kind. How do we start over?

Even if we're comfortable and content with our significant other, and things are going relatively well between us, the one answer to all four of these questions still applies. In fact, our ability to see the truth of it is what determines whether our love will have what it needs to flourish or if it withers on the vine. Please give the following insight all the attention it deserves:

The longing we have to love and be loved is *not* some fixed bond that, once made between consenting partners, forever answers our need for love. *For love to flourish it must be ceaselessly exchanged.* Like the pristine waters of a high mountain stream, if love isn't renewed it ceases to flow, stagnates, and eventually disappears.

Our own personal experience proves this last insight. It helps explain why we find ourselves looking into the eyes of those we love as we seek—in a wordless communication—a feeling of love that we both need, and want to share with our partner. So that when we do say, "I love you"—or give some unspoken affection to a child, or even a cherished pet that returns our gaze—what we're really saying is, *right here, right now,* being with you completes the need I have to love and to feel loved. And as our love is renewed, so are we. But we also know that our relationships aren't always made up of these tender moments and their sweet mercies.

In this book you will discover how to use the "not so good, maybe bad, and even ugly moments" with your partner to deepen, strengthen, and refresh the love between you. *That's* real relationship magic: being able to transform the "straw that might break the camel's back" into a nugget of gold that enriches both of you at the same time.

In This Book You Will Learn How To:

1. Use whatever differences there are between you and your partner to become more loving and kind with one another.

2. Bring any argument to a dead stop, and deepen the bond between you and your partner *at the same time*.

3. Love your partner *fully*—without the fear of loss—in spite of failed or painful relationships in the past.

4. Break those old patterns where "push comes to shove" with your partner, turning your relationship into a dark merry-go-round.

But be warned: doing the inner work it takes to start waking up together is *not* for the faint of heart, nor are they for anyone who still believes there may be a "good" reason to have a knock-down, drag-out fight with their partner.

What you're about to read has no familiar platitudes or affirmations to be used *after* you and your partner crash into one another and start throwing around the blame for who did what to whom.

Instead you're about to discover a profound set of higher principles that—once understood and put into practice—will not only help to heal the hurts and misunderstandings that lie at the root of all your relationship problems, but also eventually empower you to *stop any fight before it begins*.

Solve These Most Daunting Relationship Mysteries

1. Why are we drawn into certain relationships, especially to those that are "bad" for us?

2. Do we really attract opposites into our life? Is there such a thing as a soul mate, and is there a way to know if I've found mine?

3. Why do so many relationships often end up in a mess, and what can I do to ensure this doesn't happen to me and my partner?

4. How can I help my partner outgrow certain undesirable parts of their character that constantly get under my skin?

The special answers to these questions, and many, many more just like them, will give you the new knowledge and specific actions you need to build a vibrant relationship that very few people ever have the good fortune to experience; a relationship that is self-refreshing, spontaneously fun, deeply affectionate, incorruptible, and above all truly loving.

The Best Way to Read This Book

I decided to call this book *Relationship Magic* because in one respect it is just that…magic. But I don't mean the kind of magic that you see performed on a stage, or for that matter any action or ritual perceived as belonging to some arcane craft or practice.

In truth, it wasn't that long ago that much of what we see in our everyday lives today would have been taken for some form of magic: being able to look inside a human body using a device to reveal its subtle systems, talking over great distances by speaking into an instrument worn on our wrist, creating synthetic diamonds or medicines by manipulating their molecular structure. All of these things that would have been considered magic in the world of yesteryear are common to us today.

I take the pains to make this point because there will be some things in this book that may seem impossible to do. However, let me assure you of two things: first, it wasn't the passage of time that made what might have once been called magical into part of our everyday experience; it just took this passage of time to reveal all of the "magic" already hidden in it. This is also true when it comes to the magic of love. It's not just waiting for the right conditions to let it unfold; all of its possibilities are already within us. Let me explain this important idea.

What seems impossible to one level of consciousness— unconditional patience, kindness, and compassion—is, in fact, natural to a higher level of our own self. So that just as our past obviously already contained the "magical" knowledge we would need to transform that understanding into the incredible devices we use today, so within us lives the "magic" of a love yet to be manifested within us.

And that's why I have written this book: to help you discover that everything you need to know—the higher self-knowledge that transforms any unwanted moment with your partner into one of unconditional love—*already lives within you*. And, as an inextricable, seemingly inexplicable part of this discovery process, to help you see—in real time—the fact that *your partner is exactly who you need to realize this infinite possibility*.

So you and I are about to set on a very special kind of journey, which is why I subtitled this book *Waking Up Together*. It is an adventure, and a great one at that!

Still, as is true with entering into any new territory, you need to be prepared for what you will see. That's why I strongly suggest that your first time through the book you read it one chapter at a time in the order they are written. However, after you finish reading the entire book, feel free to open it anywhere at any time, and you will find the lesson you need just waiting for you.

A Quick Look Into the Book of Relationship Magic

Each of the ten chapters is a level of study in itself, like the rungs of a ladder that you stand on when reaching for something just above your present grasp. In this instance, we take one step at a time, consolidating our new and higher understanding even as we leave our former, and more limited, level of understanding behind us.

In chapter 1, *How to Realize the Invisible Promise and Power of Love,* you will be introduced to some of the broad but more important celestial laws that govern our relationships. The ideas it covers are designed to help you gain the basic understanding you'll need to build on all the lessons that follow.

In chapter 2, *The Tao of Love*, you'll learn how and why painful relationships are born, the truth about the "law of attraction," and how to turn whatever you oppose in your partner into the realization of a higher order of love.

Each of the remaining eight chapters will take you a rung higher, which means the ideas are designed to build on one another. With each step up, you will see farther and farther, making you freer not just to give love, but to be loved as well.

In chapter 3, *Three Revelations to Help You Rediscover the Power of Love*, you're introduced to the unseen force that pushes people apart, and why before you can hope to have a better relationship with your partner, you're going to need a better understanding of yourself. You'll also be shown how to use difficult moments with your partner to strengthen your relationship.

In the fourth chapter, *Start Taking Full Responsibility for Your Relationship,* you'll learn the secret of how to keep any passing negative "mood" from spoiling your relationship or punishing your partner. You will also be shown how—by taking conscious responsibility for your own interior state—you can stop any fight midstream, turning an unpleasant moment into one full of new possibilities.

In chapter 5, *The Secret of Making a Fresh Start*, you will be given "new eyes" to see why compromising yourself for the sake of some makeshift peace with your partner *never* works. You'll also learn how to release yourself and your partner from repeating those familiar painful patterns. Most significantly, you'll be introduced to five powerful words that can bring any moment of conflict between you and your partner to an instantly *positive* end.

In chapter 6, *Your Relationship Can Only Be as New as You Are Willing to Be,* you'll gain insight into the real and unseen cause behind petty and big arguments alike, including a two-step process that will show you how to turn these unwanted events into a powerfully healing moment for both of you.

As you might imagine, the lessons in this chapter, which are just about halfway up the ladder, are a bit more challenging. But never forget the following, particularly when it comes to understanding the remainder of the book and your work to implement its practices: *with love, all things are possible.*

In the seventh chapter, *Take the Upper Path That Leads to Perfect Love,* we come upon a remarkable discovery about our partner guaranteed to "take the fight" out of us every time we're able to realize the truth of it. We also learn all about a higher order of compassion that's capable of closing any distance—of healing any pain—that may have come to drive us apart from those we love.

In chapter 8, *The Awakening of a Selfless Love That Encompasses All,* we gain precious insight into a higher order of love that effortlessly casts off any residual pain of resentment or regret that runs through our relationships. We're also given three new intentions to work with that are designed to help us learn how to love our partner as we wish to be loved by them.

In the ninth chapter, *Start Making Space for Your Partner to Grow,* we look at one of the unseen ways that we unknowingly interfere with the growth of our partner, not to mention how we may be unconsciously turning them against us in these same moments. We also discover proof positive why *any* attempt on our part to change our partner "for the better" always backfires.

Finally, in chapter 10, *The ABCs of Relationship Magic,* we find out just how counterproductive it is to blame our partner for any pain we want to blame on them. We're given two powerful exercises—real-time practices on our part that are designed to allow our partner the space they need to succeed in realizing their highest possibilities. We also see why the only way to perfect the love between us requires that we practice that love *until it perfects us.*

One last thought about this journey of love, and all of the beautiful laws you're about to learn in order to be a better partner to the one you love:

In a perfect world, you might read this book with your partner. That would be ideal. You would discuss the principles and how they may or may not apply to your partnership. You'd share the insights discovered from working through the exercises with one another. And, perhaps most important of all, you would both see how these revelations are working to deepen the love you have for one another, effortlessly raising the quality of your relationship.

Yes, I realize your partner may not be ready for this kind of journey, and so the above may not yet be possible; in fact, it's probably not likely at all. But...that's okay, and here's why:

You are the one who senses the infinite possibilities of love.

You are the one who has glimpsed—no matter how dimly it may be—that love can't grow in the shadow of any bitterness, regret, or resentment.

You are the one whose heart is grateful for the love you have, but who also somehow knows there is no end to the journey before the two of you...if only you will honor the higher part of yourself that senses this beautiful possibility.

And if the above is true, then it means—at least for a little while—that *you* will have to be the first to change.

You will have to lead by example, even when you're not quite sure what that "best" example might be. Still, all that said, if you study the insights in this book with the wish to understand them, and then practice the lessons in higher love that they underpin, *you* will change. I can guarantee this because I know that the magic of love is already living within you. It just needs someone who will dare to realize it. Do this, and as you are transformed by the power of love, your partner will see changes happening to you that they can't understand...but that they will want to. And so you will lead them to change as well.

Promises between you will no longer be necessary because you will be *showing* them the love you want them to share with you.

Here are just a few of the important discoveries that you're about to make as you set out on this journey of waking up together. Consider the following seven key lessons as a kind of "sneak preview" of the heart-healing, relationship-enriching principles to be studied, in depth, in the pages that follow.

1. The real problem we have with others is what we don't yet see and understand about *ourselves.*

2. It makes no difference to whom, or at what, we point the finger of pain to blame for our suffering, because until we become aware *of our own hand* in these unwanted moments...nothing can change.

3. It's not by ignoring the differences between our partner and ourself that we get past how they "rub" us wrong, but rather by learning to use them—as does the jeweler his polishing wheel—to help perfect both of us, not only as lovers and friends, but also as individuals.

4. When it comes to being partners with the one we love...any time we fight, *each of us* is responsible for whatever may be happening to *both* of us.

5. Despite any appearance to the contrary, it's not our partner, nor is it we who strike the first blow in any dispute: *It's pain that picks the fight.*

6. Our negative reactions have no awareness of themselves at all, which means that not only are they blind, but they are also incapable of loving anything.

7. If we will do our part, love will do the rest... but we must choose to put it to the test. With love, all things are possible.

One Way to See the "Magic" Come Alive in You

I remember as a boy watching my friend do a magic trick. At the time it seemed incredible, but I was likely easily impressed. So, I asked him to teach me the trick.

"Oh no," he said; "a magician never gives away his secrets." There was only one thing left for me to do... I went to the same magic store where he picked up the trick, and I bought the same one for myself. Here's the moral of this little story:

What good is magic that someone else can do, but that you can't? So let me tell you about a little magic that you can do with this book, but only if you follow these instructions I'm about to give you.

There's little doubt that as you read through the world of new ideas you're about to discover in this book, you will run into a few places that you don't quite understand, or that you want to understand more deeply, but can't.

First, this is natural; it's expected. So just read over those passages and take from them what you can. Mark these parts of the book using a highlighter, or make a note about that page and place. Then just move on, giving no more thought to that temporary stumbling block whatsoever.

Then, once you've read through the whole book, go back to these places that may have confused you—and now, here's the magic I promised that you would see: the parts of the book that gave you pause before will tell you their secrets because *you will be looking at them with brand-new eyes.* The ideas and insights that you may have initially stumbled over will be magically transformed into a ladder whose steps lead you to a world of higher self-understanding.

1

How to Realize the Invisible Promise and Power of Love

It's not something most of us would admit to, at least not openly...but, nevertheless, it's true: when it comes to many of our relationships—with family, friends, or lovers—or even a simple encounter with a stranger on the street—there often come times when a little "push" turns into a "shove." And before we know it, we've either hurt someone we didn't mean to, or...we've been hurt and beat a retreat. No judgment here. We've all been there, done that...and not just once! For the most part, it may all seem fairly innocent. But, behind the curtain of each incident, something is growing in us that guarantees the only change we can look forward to in our relationships with others is what we blame each other for. Here's why.

Despite our best intentions, these conflicts have a strong tendency to repeat themselves. Before we even know it, certain painful patterns get formed. We're more and more easily moved to act in anger, or to speak out of frustration. And so it comes to pass: with each iteration of this irritation—each time we feel "rubbed" the wrong way—a kind of callus slowly forms around our heart. This kind of hardening seems innocent enough; it grows "naturally," much in the same way as do stalactites in a cave.

We've all seen what these strangely shaped structures look like, either in a book or on film. They hang like dark-colored icicles from the roof of a cave; and, to the point, they are formed by calcium salts slowly being deposited on them—layer by layer—by the steady drip of mineral-enriched waters.

With this image in mind, consider the slow but steady "drip" of feeling disappointed, betrayed, or disrespected by another. Can we see the parallel? Each negative reaction to some unwanted moment in one of our relationships has a distinct, but very similar, effect.

Slowly but surely, we form a kind of shell within and around ourselves to keep from being hurt again. But, while this self-protective layer *seems* to insulate us from further emotional injury, it accomplishes this dark undertaking at a terrible cost to us; in truth, to all whom we might ever care for.

It should be obvious, but it's not: *we can't protect our heart and keep it open at the same time,* any more than it's possible to be covered by a shadow and feel the caress of a sunbeam touch our face.

The more we unknowingly agree to be guarded by these shadows of old fears and lingering regrets, the less chance we have of experiencing the unexpected delight of discovering and exploring something new...not just in our partner, but within ourselves as well.

Imagine a young child who can't understand why a small, beautiful potted rose their parent gave them to keep on the ledge of their bedroom window has stopped growing; even worse, it's started to wilt. Nothing they do to nurse it back to health works. They don't want their parent to know; they're afraid, maybe embarrassed that something's wrong with *them*.

Fortunately, the parent is able to see that something's troubling their child, and soon discovers the withering rose that has been hidden. The parent smiles and explains to the child:

"Little one, you've done nothing wrong; we will soon make things right. Your rose has stopped growing because its roots have outgrown the original pot in which I gave it to you. If you want it to be healthy and happy, to be able to keep growing, we have to move it into a larger pot, which I'll be glad to help you do."

When it comes to relationships that are feeling stunted, too well worn, or somehow too wearing on us—where we may be trying to hide how we feel, or blaming ourselves for some failure—we need a similar solution as just illustrated above: what we need is a bigger "pot."

Just as a rose can't survive and thrive when its roots are confined, neither can our relationships flower in a like situation. Only in this case it's our heart that's contained, stuck behind a wall of preconceived notions that don't just create limitations in our relationships, but that also keep it locked out of the love it longs for above all else. Let's explore this last crucial idea.

Revealed: The Unseen Limitation to Love Without Limit

As we are going to learn in the chapters ahead, *there is no* inherent *limitation in any relationship to which we are drawn or that we attract to ourselves.*

In fact, one of the reasons we are drawn to others is precisely because in his or her presence we feel new possibilities in ourselves that we can't wait to explore! Which means, the real limitation is not due to some imagined inability to love unconditionally. It is not the "other one" who just "doesn't get it," and neither are we stuck in some contradictory set of circumstances. If any of the above were true, we would be out of luck; it would mean our ability to love freely, to give ourselves completely, is limited to conditions beyond our control. As we will see, this is not true.

The real underlying limitation in our relationships is rooted in how we look at and think about others who are in our life. But, perhaps more accurately stated, *the real problem we have with others is what we don't yet see and understand about ourselves!* Here's just one example:

One of the big things that *really* troubles us about others is that they just don't "measure up"—at least in that troubled moment—to *our* expectations of them. In our eyes, they have failed to "complete" us *as we had imagined is their responsibility*. Let's take a moment to really consider this last idea. Is it really his or her failure to perform as "assigned" that's making us feel unhappy, or ... is the real limitation our unseen false belief that others are responsible for how we feel?

This false belief, that "your" purpose in life is to ensure that "I" remain contented, pleased with our relationship, literally chokes the life ... and the love out of it.

It's critical we look at the above idea through the lens of our past experiences with others, in particular as it regards those we may have loved and hurt, or who we feel have hurt us. Only then will we be able to see how this misunderstanding can't do anything but mangle our relationships by creating—as it must—a false, but fierce dependency upon others. The facts that follow pretty much speak for themselves.

The greater our dependency on others to provide us with a sense of self-worth, or to see ourselves in their eyes as being special and unique, the more we feel some form of resentment building up in us when, as passing time always inevitably proves, they fail to meet our expectations.

This pent-up resentment usually leads to an outburst of some kind, fueled by frustration or anger toward them. Of course, attending these heated moments—that can't take place without their company—are those too familiar thoughts and feelings "telling" us we really have no choice but to "correct" that person. After all, he or she has failed to fulfill the role that we assigned to them in that relationship. Again, past experience proves the point: could we feel this kind of disappointment with someone's behavior if we hadn't first harnessed them to the "yoke and plow" of our own perfect expectations? There's no other good explanation for our negative reaction toward a partner—let alone someone we may have just met—other than an unseen false belief that nothing they do in life is supposed to disturb us! And, in case this isn't abundantly clear, as long as we believe that anyone else is responsible for our sense of well-being, we feel it's our right to keep spurring them on until they get it right!

To summarize: the more we lean on some relationship—to fulfill any false purpose unknowingly appointed to it—the more such demands not only blind us, but they secretly serve to bind us to something worse: they keep us from realizing *the real purpose*—the magic—hidden in each and every relationship that comes into our life, something we will now look at together.

All of our relationships are a kind of mirror; they serve us somewhat in the same way as does the bedroom mirror before which we dress when getting ready to leave the house. Its reflection lets us see how we look, and decide if we like how we feel about what we've put on that day.

Standing before the mirror of our relationships—a ceaseless reflection of that relationship as it unfolds—we are given to see something about *who we are* in that same moment. In this way each relationship serves to reveal to us something we may have not yet realized as being true about our present nature. In other words, whenever I'm around "you" there's the prospect of being introduced to a "me"—parts of myself—*that I may have not yet met!* Here's an example of this powerful idea, and how it works its magic in us.

Maybe we're on a nature hike where we round a bend, suddenly finding ourselves standing at the foot of a towering waterfall. It's majestic. A delicate mist covers everything, catching the sunlight, creating a million tiny prisms of colored light.

There's never been such a moment for us because *we have never been who we are in that same instant.* In such moments we are filled with an incomparable sensation that is one and the same as meeting a whole new level of our own being.

Or, perhaps we look up to see an unending night sky, and in our relationship with that dark expanse we experience the feeling of something deep and vast within us; we sense the presence of something eternal. In that moment, we are given a glimpse of something we would never see otherwise: the timelessness we feel stirring in us ... has *always* lived in us.

Much as, in the fairy tale, Sleeping Beauty is awakened from her deep sleep by the "kiss" of Prince Charming, so can all of our relationships—with everyone, *with anyone*—serve to stir us awake, not only that we might experience some deeper, truer, sense of self, but so that through that same awakening we may touch and be touched by a higher order of love that can be realized in no other way.

The Magnificent Magnetics of Love

Have you ever wondered why you can feel so drawn, attracted, to someone you've just met, or how much you can instantly dislike a person ... even just meeting him or her for the first time! Why are we drawn to one person, and opposed to another, often for no apparent reason?

What could be more mysterious than these unseen forces at work within us that govern how we respond and relate to one another? For instance, when it comes to love, or as regards any of our relationships with others, why do "opposites attract"?

And while we're on the subject of this strange attraction, let's broaden the scope of our study: for the infinite number of possibilities—or, as my mother used to say, out of "all the fish in the sea"—what is it that draws us to enter into those specific relationships whose influences literally help shape our destiny?

One main reason for the strong attraction we feel toward those who are special to us is that when we're with them, they "move" us like no one else can; they literally awaken in us wonderful thoughts and feelings ordinarily inaccessible to us through any of our other relationships. We all know something of these feelings; perhaps we've even told someone, "I love the way you make me feel." And let it also be noted here that these kinds of feelings don't just apply to relationships with significant others. We are also granted a similar special awareness of ourselves when we watch a loving mother care for her newborn baby, when we see a puppy chase its own tail, or when we stand in a field of wildflowers as their petals reflect the morning sun.

A Look at the "Dark Side" of Love

As marvelous as these moments are to which we feel drawn—for all the reasons just described—they are only *half* of a greater, even more magical story.

The other half of this story that's almost impossible to understand is that the exact same set of laws is at work when we attract "relationships of the unwanted kind." Think of those strained encounters where, for reasons that defy any kind of logic, we draw certain disagreeable people or conditions into our life beyond our capacity to control, or even escape.

And so we see this other side of the law of attraction as being negative, because the strange nature of its power is the exact opposite of what we'd prefer: it draws unwanted "visitors" that—no matter how many times we tell them to go away and leave us alone—just keep showing up at our door!

But if we can shake ourselves free from the prison of our own preconceived notions as to the nature of this mysterious magnetic force whose work in us so totally confounds us, we will discover something genuinely miraculous. These seemingly opposing roles serve the same great purpose: to help us awaken to and realize a higher order of unconditional love that doesn't just live within us, but that we live within as well.

Perhaps you're asking, "How can this be? What possible good is there in my unwanted moments with others, and what has that to do with love?" A quick review of what we've learned so far … will answer this question.

We've seen the main reason we're drawn to any one particular relationship is that the more we're able to give ourselves to it, the more we're given to understand about ourselves; we realize something *only that relationship can reveal to us*.

And further, that in each of these "revealing" moments—where we're shown some otherwise inaccessible truth about ourselves—we also experience a kind of profound healing because of it. Some unknown part of us that maybe, just a moment before, felt incomplete is now made whole. This is easy to see: love's power to "reveal" is also her power to help heal. Love doesn't just integrate us; she shows us that these missing parts of us weren't really missing at all—they had just been asleep. Now let's apply this same understanding and look at what seems like the "dark side" of love.

Just as we're unable to realize our own highest possibilities without love's quickening touch awakening us to them, so it is when it comes to love's "opposite" action in our life. We must also be awakened to see and realize the unconscious parts of us, living in the "dark" of us, that stand directly in the way of love's healing revelations.

We all know some of these characters. Perhaps it's a fear of being hurt again, or a mistrust of others that has run so deep it cuts love down before it has any chance to flower. Whatever its name or quality, *any negative thought or feeling that hides within us must be revealed before it can be healed.* And that's just the point; love illuminates these characters that live in the dark of us, releasing us from their unseen limitations.

So here's what we have come to see: the forces of love express themselves in equal, but opposite, ways. One side of love is active; it feels largely positive to us as it serves to reveal and affirm in us what we wish to realize as true. It strengthens our hope and faith in a power greater than ourselves that we see must be shared before it can become fully our own.

The other side of love is passive; it feels mostly negative to us because it reveals self-limiting parts of us, still at large in the dark of us. It illuminates stumbling blocks so that they can be seen as the obstacles to love that they are. Were it not for the often-painful revelation of these limitations in us, we would never see the need to release them, let alone be free to love without fear or reservation.

2

The Tao of Love

Who hasn't wondered about that age-old wisdom as concerns love and life…that "opposites attract"? Mostly we want to know, how does this law apply to me? Does it mean that whatever, or whomever, I feel drawn to is my opposite? And does this same law—that "opposites attract"—also apply to whatever, or whomever, I attract into my life?

To put it mildly, there's a lot of confusion surrounding these celestial laws of attraction. So, let's drill down a bit and see what we can learn about this strange kind of "magnetism" that makes our world "go round." Discovering the real answers we need demands the following brief but simple lesson in elementary physics.

Everything in creation—all that comes into existence with each passing moment—is the manifestation of three principle forces. This is a scientific fact that also verifies what saints and sages have always taught as being true throughout time: there are "golden threads" of unconditioned energies that don't just weave their way through everything we see, sense, and feel, but that sit, invisibly, as the forces behind the grand tapestry of life itself.

In the West, these three forces are identified by the role they play in creation: one is called "active," its partner force is called "passive," and the third of these forces is called a "modifying" or reconciling force. Let's look at a simple example of their ceaseless interplay by calling up a common experience in our everyday life:

You're at a party, standing on one side of the room. People are all around you, but you turn your gaze and put your attention on a person on the other side of the room; your energy is, for the moment, "active."

Almost magically, he or she looks back at you. They have felt, "passively," the active touch of your attention upon them.

Now a third force comes into play as both of you become increasingly aware of what's unfolding in that moment. In the other person, a flood of associations—promising or punishing in nature depending on past similar situations—coalesce into a reaction. Whatever form this reaction takes—whether to smile at you, or to quickly look away—is how the tension created by the meeting of these active and passive forces is reconciled. And so the story continues to unfold...

This same idea of three creative forces, known by many as the "trinity," is the foundation of most, if not all, of the great religions. Most of us are familiar with the idea of the Father, the Son, and the Holy Ghost. This trinity represents the three created aspects or "persons" of the One Divine Life from out of which these celestial forces emerge to oversee the grand cycle of creation: life, death, and rebirth.

We don't have to look too far or too deep to see the theme of a trinity as it appears and runs through virtually all the world's great religions, including those spiritual traditions that the passage of time has all but erased. According to the early Catholic theologian St. Jerome, "All the ancient nations believed in the Trinity."[2] A brief history will help establish this fact.

In ancient Sumeria, the universe was divided into three principle domains, each governed by its particular divinity: Anu watched over the sky; Enlil, the earth; and Ea, the waters. Together, they acted as one; three forces-in-one, as needed to establish and oversee creation.

The ancient Babylonians recognized the doctrine of "three persons" in one God, and used the equilateral triangle as an emblem of this Trinity in unity.

In India, the three gods in one are Brahma, the creator; Vishnu, the preserver; and Siva, the destroyer.

---

2. Marie Sinclair, Countess of Caithness, *Old Truths in a New Light* (London: Chapman and Hall, 1876).

In Buddhism, there is the Trikāya doctrine: the three bodies of Buddha, responsible for existence, experience, and its perfection.

Of course, there are more examples we could cite here but, for now—and to see just how these three forces work to help create and shape the relationships we have with one another—we will turn our attention to the Tao, an ancient Chinese school of spiritual thought whose teaching has been conveyed through time by a symbol most of us recognize:

This image depicting the concept of Tao portrays the existence of twin celestial powers responsible, in part, for creation: they are, as we discussed, active and passive forces. A quick study of this symbol will give us invaluable insight into the unique characteristics of the forces it portrays.

One side of the symbol represents darkness, the other side, light; in other terms, night and day; emptiness and fullness; so on and so forth.

These forms are called "yang" and "yin." They are "opposites" that secretly complement and complete one another in a ceaseless dance. To help understand this important idea, think of the systolic and diastolic actions of your own heart; what we think of as our heartbeat is really one side of it emptying itself, even as the other side is filled as a result. These seemingly opposing movements are not just ceaselessly interacting with one another but, in their ceaseless turning round each other, work together to create the possibility of a greater whole: life!

Everything that breathes, from a microorganism to the expansion and contraction of a star, is subject to these celestial laws. And the marriage, or the reconciliation of these opposing forces—that allows them to act in concert for a purpose greater than either of them alone—is made possible by the presence of a third power, a grand force that encircles and unites them for a single grand purpose: to give birth to a wholly new form that is conceived from the union of the opposites. And all begins again.

Perhaps you're thinking, "What on earth has all of this to do with learning to love without limit? What have these principles to do with learning the secrets of relationship magic?" As we're about to discover, everything. So, let's see.

For most of us, our immediate reaction to the idea of "opposing forces" in any relationship brings up painful images and unwelcome feelings, like reliving the misery of old arguments with partners past ... or still present.

And then there's the aftermath of remembering how often mom and dad, friends, or family members would fight over opposing views of how things should be. So ingrained are the memories of these unwanted moments—their strain, including the fear of having to relive anything like them again—that the idea being proposed here, i.e., that opposing forces are secretly complementary, may seem impossible.

Let's look at a couple of these common examples where it feels as if life itself opposes our happiness and peace of mind. None can deny the repeated experience of these daily conditions that seem set against us:

1. The familiar struggle between friends, family, and partners: *what I want,* that you don't—or—*what you want,* that I don't.

2. The unwanted event: any offhand comment by someone that cuts like a knife, that crushes our expectations and seems set against our best interests.

These are common enough examples. Anything anyone does that opposes, or otherwise challenges, some image we may have of ourselves is met with an immediate knee-jerk negative reaction. But the key here to understand is that our experience of the moment—how we feel as these relationships unfold—*is one hundred percent determined by our perception of them* in that exact same instant. Again, we can use our own experience to prove the point. When our partner of the moment is stimulating, exhilarating, or finds us irresistible in some way, we have great pleasure being in their company. Whoever may be flattering us is just about perfect!

On the other hand, woe be it unto anyone who "messes" with us; meaning, if you at all seem to judge, criticize, or stand in the way of my wishes or wants—especially as concerns my expectations of your role in them—then there's only one thing left to do: *straighten you out!*

We know this "drill"…where we do whatever we feel we must to make our partner get in line with our demand; or, failing that, make them pay for their misstep! But, much as we're all familiar with this strategy—designed to bring an end to our pain by holding our partner responsible for it—we also seem to be painfully unaware of the following fact:

Blaming, or struggling to control, the other person *never* works. Not really. These tactics, even when they seem effective, change nothing. Even if we seem to win that argument, all we've really done is temporarily postpone that inevitable conflict that comes knocking the next time someone or something steps up to oppose us.

Add to this situation the fact that *there can be no dispute between two people unless each feels wronged by the other*, and we can see why our resentment toward the offending other keeps growing. And when this pressure can no longer be contained, the next fight—likely a feud over some reason more trivial than the one before it—is usually twice as heated.

But, startling though it may be, at least at first, here's the fact: It's *not* our partner—whether it's our brother, mother, supervisor, grocery clerk, or lover—who needs to be fixed. As hard as it may be to understand in the heat of some struggle with another: *they* are not "broken." To be clear, we are all in the same "fix." We've lost our connection with a higher order of love; one that's not only intended to help nourish our relationships with each other, but that keeps showing us unlimited ways we can use our relationships—even the most troubling of them—to become a better, more loving human being. This may seem, at first, anyway, like an idea too big to consider, but we can learn to see these celestial laws at work in the most common of things.

Think of a flower, her soft petals exposed to the light of the sun. She is passive to the active radiance that nourishes her, even as she turns her face to follow the life-giving light. Here we see two seemingly separate forms and forces, each an expression of a different level of existence: the sunlight, pressing down and in, and the flower, rooted in the earth, open and receptive to its life-giving touch. The union of these forces is an act of creation, and from their marriage the purpose of that flower is fulfilled. And standing there, petals illumined in full display, its beauty catches the eye of someone walking by who stops and admires this "simple" wildflower, grateful for the gift of seeing it. This is the Tao of Love at work.

When the Student Is Ready, Relationships Appear to Teach

Our experience of any relationship—whether it's with brother, mother, dad, partner, or lover—can't be separated from the level of our present understanding about the purpose of the same. We've already touched a bit on this important idea, but a little refresher will ensure the next section of this chapter hits the mark.

One of the reasons we like falling in love—or meeting and making new friends—is that these relationships come with little to no baggage. But while these new relationships come with no troublesome backstory…it isn't too long before they start to look—and feel—very similar to all of our other relationships.

Like some plague we can see our "old story" sweep in and start to overwrite what we hoped would be a new narrative. Before too long, faultfinding becomes easier than forgiving them. The same old blame game begins, and what was new slowly takes on the appearance of what has always been. *That's why we need a whole new story,* beginning with an introduction to the following set of new and higher principles. Your careful consideration of these insights will not only prove it's possible to see all of your relationships through a brand-new set of eyes but, as you learn to embrace their wisdom, they will also help teach you, in real time, the truth about unconditional love.

As we illustrated, active and passive forces have distinct, opposing characteristics; and yet, when they're brought together, they serve not just to complement one another but to bring forth, out of their union, a new life: the "birth" of a creation that can come into existence in no other way. Nowhere is this principle more evident than when it comes to the first major distinction between the opposites as manifested in nature; here they represent "male" and "female" forces.

The Tao calls these forces yang and yin, accordingly. But, even as they manifest themselves in separate, distinct forms, i.e., as "man" and "woman," it's important to remember that—spiritually speaking—neither the male nor female attribute exists apart from its opposite; in other words, *their existence is mutually dependent.* And yet—from the union of these "opposing" forces, and the forms they embody—is conceived something that is greater than the sum of its parts.

With these ideas in mind, let's examine a little more closely some of the finer elements that comprise these "male" and "female" characteristics. But, before we move ahead, let's be crystal clear about the following: when it comes to how these opposites express themselves in life, neither is "superior" to the other. And regardless of how either may temporarily express itself, of itself it has no dark or negative connotation.

Yin is the female principle; she is the passive force of creation. But passive doesn't mean "weak," any more than a riverbed is subservient to the waters that rush through it. Without such a bed, and its banks, there is no river.

Yin abides as does a dark, deeply shaded valley; in one respect she represents a void, an emptiness; pure potential waiting for perfect conception. To help you see this principle, think of when a potter first starts working with a handful of clay. It is void of form; the clay is purely passive, waiting for the active hands of the potter to bring forth any one of its infinite possibilities. Gradually, from this union of clay and sculpting hands, is formed a beautiful cup, bowl, or vase—yet another form of emptiness, waiting to be filled with tea, soup, or beautiful flowers.

Now, returning briefly to the image of our deep-shaded valley, can we see—through this same metaphor—that this expression of yin is "waiting" to be filled, ready to take into itself the warmth of the sun as it rises to pour itself in? And that the light that pierces its darkness brings with it the energy it needs to sustain and complete the cycle of life in this valley. Again, we are speaking of complementary forces.

In real life, nothing exists just for itself. What is active can't be complete without something to "touch," as surely as what is passive can't be made whole without being "touched." And as these forces intermingle, "touching" one another, they complete the need and purpose of the other through that touch. This is a description of an ancient art called tantric sex: a vital relationship between male and female forces, where, through a prolonged act of sexual intercourse—(including the discipline this requires)—active and passive forces are brought to rest within each other. Through the participants' conscious union of these forces, they are elevated and transported into the flow of an exalted, sublime state of undivided energy.

All that we have been studying and learning together up until now has been to help us reach and see this singular point: *we are not the sole creators of the relationships we have with those who come into our lives, or those into whose lives we are drawn.* There is a much bigger story here, and the better we are able to understand it, the more fulfilled we find ourselves in each and all of our relationships.

From the moment of birth, our life is the expression of a greater, invisible relationship that precedes it. We are, at once, the instrument of a host of invisible celestial forces even as we are instrumental in *their* concerted work to create, express, and ultimately restore within us—and in our relationships, respectively—the harmony of the heavens from out of which these forces come. To prove that these last few thoughts are not "pie in the sky," let's look at a simple example of the grand design behind these "opposing" forces, and how we can use them to discover real relationship magic.

The essence of yin is "female," primarily emotional; a reservoir of intuitive feelings, her character is communicative. She is dependent but only in the sense of being able to wait, passively, patiently, upon whatever is needed to complete her. She is "other-centered."

On the other hand, yang is "male" in essence, primarily intellectual, reliant on reason. His nature is independent, prone to silence, while actively seeking to possess what is thought necessary to complete him. He is "self-centered."

She wants him to feel what—and as—she does, to enter into her space and share all that resides in the secret depths of her nature.

He wants her to give him space, to understand his needs without him ever having to speak of them.

We have to ask ourselves: what on earth could draw such opposing forces to come together, and for what purpose? After all, we know—generally speaking—what happens when these kinds of opposing forces meet head to head, and it's not always pretty! So, what's going on here?

Love has drawn these opposing forces together so that they might be united in an act that fulfills the higher purpose for which they are created: that they might complete one another. What does this event look like in "real time"?

Let's take a look at just one of the ways this higher principle could play itself out. Maybe you've seen something like the following scenario unfold in one of your own relationships:

Perhaps he sees that she's suffering because of his unseen self-absorbed thinking, or over some equally self-centered action. Almost instantly he becomes aware—maybe for the first time—that her pain can be directly attributed to a certain characteristic of his in which—prior to this moment—he had always taken pride. This revelation comes as a real shock to his ego; he is awakened, suddenly mindful of what had been—only a heartbeat before—a blind, unconscious, and inconsiderate force in him. But... now he sees this characteristic for what it is: a major stumbling block standing between them... a real barrier to any further development of their relationship. And so, for the sake of the love that brought them together, he realizes that it is he who must change; and not just for her, but also to answer his now obvious need to outgrow a part of himself that he's seen, firsthand, is set against him and his own highest possibilities.

Can we see how perfectly these seemingly opposing pieces come together to create a possibility greater than any one of them would have by itself? After all, were it not for these contrasting characteristics between him and his partner, he would have never been made conscious of the parts of himself that—on one hand—are in the way of the love he seeks, but that on the other hand, he had to realize in order to fulfill love's higher purpose for him! Such a beautiful mystery! Their seeming differences, understood properly, become the very force that serves to reveal, and then heal, whatever may have been in the way of this couple taking the next step in realizing unconditional love. This is relationship magic.

An Inside Look at the Secret Magic of Love

When all is said and done, the greatest stories of all time—the true classics, though not commonly seen as such—are all love stories.

Perhaps you're thinking, "That isn't so. What about something like Dickens' *A Christmas Carol*, or Hugo's *Les Miserables*? After all, not *every* classic is like *Titanic*, or *Romeo and Juliet*. How about *12 Angry Men* or *The Shawshank Redemption*, not to mention *Schindler's List*?"

What makes books or films like these love stories, particularly when many of them have no obvious love interest at their core? A closer look "tells the tale."

The central figure in virtually every classic story, past and present, goes through a soul-wrenching, life-changing transformation of his or her character ... *for the sake of love*. But, as should be obvious in the titles listed above, this deep character conversion is not necessarily for the love of another person, but rather for the love of an ideal, for the sake of some timeless value whose essence is being slowly awakened in his or her heart, whose truth they can no longer ignore...even at the cost of all they formerly held as being true and valuable.

We're drawn to these stories as we are because through them, we witness the character make a great personal sacrifice of some kind, one that only a new level of conscience—as awakened by love—could make possible. We share—and remember through that story—the possibility of realizing another order of love that already lives within us, or else how could we recognize it, let alone feel as drawn to identify with it...as we are?

Let's look at a recent popular such love story through the eyes of this new understanding. It will not only empower us to see the deeper, "untold" story that lies hidden neatly between its lines but, for our discovery, also grant us invaluable insights into how to give our own love story the same happy ending.

In 1996, a romantic comedy called *Jerry Maguire* came to the "big screen." It starred Tom Cruise as a self-involved, overly confident sports agent who, during a crisis of conscience at work, writes and emails a personal "manifesto" to all his fellow agents, including the owner of the agency. In his heartfelt memo, he spells out the injustices of certain in-house practices and calls for real change in the way their business should be conducted going forward. And, for his honesty...he gets fired!

As he's walking out of the office for the last time, humiliated, he asks—thinking surely some of the other agents feel as he does—"Who will go with me? Who wants to help me start a new company, where we will do the right thing for our clients?"

A stunning silence follows. But, as he heads toward the door, one of the secretaries, Dorothy Boyd, played by Renée Zellweger, says, "Wait! I'll go with you." And together they enter into an unknown future, banking on the hope that some of his clients will make the move with him into the fold of his new company.

As it turns out, only one football player, Rod Tidwell, played by Cuba Gooding Jr., decides to go with him. This short synopsis pretty much outlines the backstory. Now let's look inside it, and see how a higher kind of love works its magic to bring about a happy ending...at all levels.

We learn that Dorothy is a single mom, and that she has nothing to fall back on if her adventure with Jerry should fail. Confounding her decision-making process, and leading to what could spell disaster, it's obvious that she has a crush on him. It's equally obvious he knows this, and that he uses her infatuation with him to ensure she goes along for the ride, despite its mounting difficulties.

It's clear: she's hoping for a "white knight" to save her from being a single mom with a young child in need of a father figure, even as he's quietly encouraging this fantasy so as to keep her close and working without a salary. What we see are two good but basically desperate people, working to salvage their individual dreams by using one another to escape their individually broken lives.

As the story line develops, including Jerry and Dorothy working their way through a couple of "make-or-break" moments in the new business, we see them not only drawing closer to one another but also gaining certain insights into each other's character.

Through the camera's eye, we see Dorothy beginning to realize Jerry's selfish motive in stringing her along, and that he is emotionally incapable of the kind of commitment she needs.

Even as all of this unfolds, Jerry continues to witness, first-hand, the deep love that his remaining star client, Rod, holds for his wife; how truly committed they are to one another. In these scenes, we see Jerry become inwardly reflective, longing to know in his own life the kind of deep love they share.

As all of these events collect and gather momentum … Dorothy gets a solid job offer in another city. This is her chance to provide herself and her son with some real security. Soon after she tells Jerry of this possibility, he asks her to marry him. It's clear he fears losing the one person left who supports his plan. But this is in no way a "happy ending." We can see each of them is only further conflicted for having forged this alliance of convenience.

Now, let's get to the heart of this story and look at the higher forces of love, of how the unseen forces of yin and yang work their invisible magic to bring about a real "happy ending"...that is just the beginning of the characters' story together.

Dorothy finally recognizes that while Jerry may be what she wants, he is—in fact—not the kind of man *she needs*. Her blind pursuit of a relationship she imagined would make her whole has blinded *her*, but now she can see what she couldn't before: she had been deceived by unseen parts of herself into compromising herself to the point of becoming someone she could no longer agree to be.

And so, in a pivotal scene, she breaks it off with him. She explains whatever it is they have together...no longer works for her. He's shocked by her decision but, because he has begun to see how dishonest he's been with her, he also knows that her choice is the right one, for both of them. At this point they part ways until a twist in the story resets the stage for a completely unexpected turn of events! In brief, here's how the rest unfolds, and then we'll study the many important lessons about *our* relationships that it holds for us.

Rod, who is Jerry's one hope for success, now playing as a free agent, makes an unbelievable touchdown catch at a crucial moment in a big game. He becomes an instant superhero to fans and coaches alike! But, in making that play, compounding the magnitude of the event—adding suspense to it—he doesn't get up from the ground; it appears he's been seriously injured. Tense moments later, we see that he's fine; but as his teammates rush to his side, now lionizing him and giving him the peer respect he's always wanted, he does the unthinkable: instead of enjoying his new celebrity, he runs into the arms of his wife who—fearful of his condition—has rushed to be by his side.

Now two things happen at once: first, Jerry, who has also rushed to the scene, seeing the adulation being poured out over his player, realizes that all his former financial worries are over; Rod has just become the new superstar he had to have to anchor his fledgling agency.

But, second, and even more moving to him, is the fact that neither Rod nor his wife seem to care for anything more in that moment than one another. He sees them in an embrace that transcends concern for money or fame. In that same moment, he feels his own heart awaken, and he realizes what he *really* wants more than anything else. So, off he goes, literally running to find Dorothy.

When he walks into her home, Dorothy's living room is filled with her lady friends. He asks to speak to her privately, but she insists that whatever he has to say should be spoken before the entire gathering.

In the following heart-warming scene—in the presence of all gathered there—Jerry struggles to find the right words. Finally, he speaks. And using just three words he conveys not just the truth of how he feels about her, but also he tells her another, much deeper kind of truth: his realization of a new level of self-understanding that he could have only attained through what their relationship had taught him.

He says to her: "*You complete me.*"

Yes, of course, all the usual ideas about the wonders of two people falling in love apply here, but there's so much more to this mystery than meets the eye. These same three simple words go right to the heart of the main lesson in this chapter that I will now spell out.

Near the end of this wonderful film, standing there with Dorothy—heart in hand—Jerry never speaks this last bit of dialogue that I've taken the license to write out just below. These few short lines not only reveal why he tells her "You complete me," but through them we also get to see what it is that is now completed in him because of their relationship.

"Were it not for you—without the strength of character you displayed when telling me that you had to let me go—because nothing good could come from living a lie—I could never have seen that all I've ever cared for is myself. *By your strength was my weakness revealed, so that I could be released from it.*"

She might say something similar to him: "Were it not for you coming into my life right when I felt so vulnerable and exposed, I could have never seen the parts of myself wanting to convince me that alone—by myself—my life amounts to nothing. Without you, *I could have never seen—let alone challenged—the false sense of dependency such a weakness lives to breed."*

The Greatest Relationship Secret of All Time

We've been studying the story line of a popular film to help us see the invisible interplay of opposing forces that are, in fact, secretly complementary; how their marriage makes it possible for us to see—and undergo—a kind of character transformation that can't come to pass in any other way.

Now, with these last important ideas in mind, let's look at a few "everyday" relationships that likely mirror some of our own. Our willingness to look closely at what they are intended to teach us about ourselves is the same as being able to realize, and then release ourselves from, whatever may be within us standing in the way of love.

Maybe we're sure that someone in our workplace is an insensitive bully, and so we tend to go the other way when we see him or her coming. We want *nothing* to do with such a relationship, but neither is there a way to "go around it," as evidenced by our inability to escape it.

Then comes that fateful day—probably when we're sick and tired of feeling that kind of fear—when a revolutionary thought pops into our mind: what if the real problem isn't that he or she can push our button... *but that we have a button that can be so easily pushed!*

In our hands now is a new understanding that changes everything, not just about that relationship, but also about who and what *we* have been up until that moment.

If it weren't for what that person manifests, that so stirs up in us what it does, we would have never known the truth that now sets us free: *what we've really been running from, all along, is the fear of our own negative reaction,* and how easily that wave of anger or resentment can carry us away. Seeing this as true gives us the strength to properly step up and challenge not only what we've taken to be our "tormentor," but also parts of ourself so easily given to feel tormented.

Here is another example where we can see how the opposites in *any* relationship can work together to create a greater good for all involved: a man can see that his girlfriend is genuinely happy for the good fortune of a mutual friend. And her joy, which he's unable to feel, let alone share with his friend, makes two things clear to him at once: not only is he cut off, unable to be happy for others, but the pain of his envy, once hidden from his sight, now becomes more than obvious. Seeing this selfish characteristic that steals what he senses should be part of his happiness in life, he goes to work to free himself of it.

In both instances, the individuals involved are given insight into some unsuspected imperfection in their heart or mind—a healing revelation that could not occur outside of the particular relationship that serves to reveal that shortfall in character. The result, assuming they are willing to receive the lessons intended for them in that moment of revelation, is to undergo a profound change in their character that can't be brought about in any other way. In exactly this manner, what had formerly been an unseen limitation is transformed into the seed of something limitless.

This is the real magic, the real power, and perhaps—in the end—the true purpose of all our relationships in life: *to help us and to help each other outgrow whatever stands in the way of perfecting our love for one another.* In other words, the differences we have with one another—including how they disturb us as they do—are as a rough gemstone to the jeweler's polishing wheel: we each exist for the sake of the other, and without one another, neither can realize our full potential.

Here's how author Thomas Moore restates this same timeless idea: "*Two people who have lived their separate lives decide to share those lives. Everyone knows the process is difficult, like crushing grapes to get the juice. But over time those raw and untested lives take on new complexity and richness, due to the sharing and the struggle. Like grape juice turning into wine, the lives ferment in an alchemy that transmutes the two from people trying to get along individually to a couple discovering the deep mystery of a shared life.*" [3]

---

3. Thomas Moore, *Writing in the Sand* (Carlsbad, CA: Hay House, 2010).

We all share a common wish: we long to be that better, truer person we know, or at least sense deep in our heart we're meant to be.

We want to be more patient, considerate, and kind to everyone we know, even to that stranger we pass on the street. By this same wish, we aspire to have the grace we know we need to love our friends, family, and partners regardless of how they may habitually disturb us. This is good.

And yet, if lofty aims could fulfill our wish to love more perfectly, we would already have, in hand, what our heart of hearts desires. Something else, something more, is needed from us if we would turn our wish into a reality.

In the coming chapters of this book you will be given the principles and practices you need to realize the beautiful, *real* possibility of being able to love without limits. More than just learning about the true nature of timeless kindness, perfect patience, and unconditional compassion, you will be shown the path that leads to a higher world within you where these timeless powers of love await anyone willing to live in that rarified air.

From this point on, each chapter of this book will end with a helpful set of questions and answers. They've been taken from real circumstances that are common sources of conflict and confusion found in many of our relationships. They are intended to shed helpful light on the subjects we've just covered.

Helpful Questions and Answers

Question: When people we love lash out at us because they are either unable or unwilling to take responsibility for their own pain, what's the best way to deal with that kind of attack? How can we support them without compromising ourselves in the act?

Answer; Assuming we have the power to do so, which is what the material in this book is intended to grant the reader, here's the best thing we can do for someone who insists that we're the source of their suffering: stop doing anything toward them that helps them think this way, including attacking them back. Here's why: when we don't defend ourselves against some cruel verbal assault, it's as if someone throws a "punch" that hits no one. Not only does our non-action leave them off balance, but it also gives them the chance to see—since we didn't "hit" back—that whatever pain they'd like to blame on us...is not because of us. Perhaps for the first time they can see that the real source of their suffering starts within them, which is also where it must end.

Question: Judging others is my problem. I comment on their looks, job, what they think, how they feel, etc. I try to stop but it's constant. What does this mean?

Answer: To one degree or another, it's our tendency to judge each other, especially when someone does something that pushes one of our buttons. But there are a couple of important things going on behind the scenes that we need to see...if we want to stop judging one another. First, all forms of judging are the same as blaming the one we judge for making us feel what we don't want to feel. But that person did not *make* us feel anything. Our task is to see that while the other may have "pushed" our button—it's *our* button! The "fingers" and the "buttons" they push are not separate things; *they don't exist without one another*. In other words, "finger" and "button" are secret opposites. The clearer we can see how the "offending" other is really just revealing the unconscious parts of ourself so easily offended, the sooner we will be free of the "judge" that lives in us.

KEY LESSONS

1. Never fight with life; your struggle is not with what opposes you, but rather with what you have yet to understand about the opposing forces that live within you.

2. Hidden within the opposing forces is a higher order of love, a celestial unity from out of which these opposites come into existence. To see the truth of this hidden relationship releases one from the bondage born of struggling with only one side or the other. Understood properly, all opposing forces contain and create their own gateway, but only when one

stands before—and within—them long enough, consciously enough, to see it open.

3. The passage of life's events, including the innumerable relationships through which they are revealed, can
either grind us down or serve to remove our rough,
sharp edges; so that whether we feel punished or are
polished by these movements all depends upon what
we love.

3

Three Revelations to Help You Rediscover the Power Of Love

In the late 1970s, I was fortunate enough to be in a small group of men and women who sat listening to an illumined human-relationship author and teacher by the name of Vernon Howard. In the years that followed—first being attracted to his work, then studying with him, and finally acting as co-director of his foundation—I came to understand…that he knew more about the nature of higher love than anyone I had ever known before, or, for that matter, would meet in the many years after.

I have taken the liberty to enlarge and enhance a few of the insights that he shared with us that day in a simple short story that follows. It reveals a very common mistake that all of us make in our search for love.

Late one evening, sitting alone in his darkened apartment, Saul is listening to a world-famous miner being interviewed on the radio. From the few details offered, it seems this man had just stumbled upon a treasure trove of some priceless gem right there in the mountains just outside the town where he lived.

In less than an hour Saul packs his camping gear, empties his pantry of canned goods, and grabs the pick and shovel that have long lain dormant in his garage. He is off to seek what he just knows will change the very course of his life … that is, once he finds it!

Ten days later, sitting around his campfire, cold, exhausted, and having spent not just all of his energy but his supplies as well, Saul is at the end of his rope. As he sits there, trying to collect his thoughts about all that's gone wrong and what he might still do to rectify his situation, he hears the sound of footsteps coming toward him from out of the dark. Who could it be?

"Hello … Is someone out there? I can't see you. Please, identify yourself. What is it you want? I have nothing of value, if that's what you're after."

"Oh no; gee, I'm sorry. I didn't mean to frighten you. I live just over the ridge, and from my balcony I saw your fire. All I wanted to do is make sure that it was a campfire out here, and nothing more dangerous."

"Sure, sure, no problem. Tell you the truth, I'm kinda glad to talk to someone. Been a while since I've had any company … other than the wolves out here. Care for a cup of coffee before you head back home? My name is Saul."

"Thank you, that sounds really good. It's a cold one tonight."

As the stranger sits down on a stone, accepting the cup of coffee that's been offered him, he can see that Saul doesn't look well at all. Everything about his physical presence appears frazzled, broken down; there seems little light in his eyes, save for the flickering of the campfire. Seeing his condition, such as it is, moves the stranger to ask a question:

"If you don't mind me asking, is everything all right? You look about as worn-out a fellow as I've ever seen. I mean, that is, if I'm not prying."

"No, you're right; things haven't gone that well...to say the least."

The stranger continues: "By the looks of how everything is all dug up around here...I take it you must be looking for something special?" And then deciding to take the risk of seeming impertinent, he finishes his thought: "But I'm guessing you haven't found it...or you wouldn't still be out here in this cold, hard place."

While a little suspicious of the questions being asked him, Saul's gratitude for the stranger's company outweighs any of his fears, so he answers: "Yeah, you're right. Been up here for about ten days, or at least I think that long. I'm looking for a very rare, incredibly valuable gemstone that I just heard has been found in this same area. But, as you've surmised, I've had no luck in finding it."

The stranger, moved by Saul's obvious plight, takes pity. "Well, if you think it would do you any good, I could come back tomorrow to help you dig around...for a little while, anyway. What's this gem supposed to look like? Can you describe it to me?"

The stranger's question sends a silent shiver coursing through Saul's entire body, but there it is. In that same instant he knows exactly why, in spite of all his hard work and sacrifice, he's not been able to find the treasure he had so hoped to claim for his own. Looking down at the ground, shaking his head, as embarrassed by what he is about to confess as he is unable to believe it true, he speaks:

"I was in such a rush to get up here, to claim one of these rare gemstones for my own, that it never even dawned on me: *I don't know what one looks like.*"

Revelation #1: What Does Love Really Look Like?

There's a healing insight hidden inside of this little story; it's a stunning idea, in many ways, but well worth our consideration if we really want to realize a love that can't be reduced to angry tears and bitter recrimination. Here it is: we don't actually know what real love "looks" like. But *we think we do*...and *that's* the problem. No one is being "judged" here, so before you jump to any conclusions, let's look at the evidence that follows. We'll see it's basically incontrovertible.

It's a rare thing, indeed, when—over time—any of our relationships live up to our expectations of them. It isn't too long before we start to feel as if "something" is missing, or even just plain wrong compared with how things were meant to unfold. And we all know the drill here: the fault is inevitably assigned to our partner. To our thinking, how can we possibly be the problem...when we're the one who's pointing it out!

Revelation #2: Love on the Rocks

Some years ago a young couple came to me, asking if I'd be willing to officiate their upcoming marriage. Their wedding was six months away, and the love they felt for one another was obvious. I had known both of them for some time, so I gladly gave my consent.

Once the planning details were out of the way, they asked if I might write some special wedding vows for them. As I listened to them speak their hearts, it was clear their love ran deep. Among other things, they wanted their promise to one another to be stated before all gathered there: "no matter what comes along, the strength of our love will always prevail."

My thoughts flashed back to a similar period of time in my life when, deeply in love, I had the exact same right feeling: love conquers all. It always has, and it always will...which, it's worth noting, happens to be true. Still, there are some lessons in life that can only be learned the "hard way." Never is this truer than when it comes to some of our most cherished ideas about this mysterious thing we call "love." So, rather than share what I felt might put a damper on their aspirations, I said nothing. We said our goodbyes, planning to speak again nearer to the big day.

About three months later I received a call from this couple, asking if I had time to speak with them about a little "problem" they were having. "Of course," I said, and we scheduled a time to meet together at a local coffee shop the next day. Here's the rundown of our conversation:

Taking turns, each reasserted how much they loved their partner, followed by a "*but* he's not 'walking the talk,'"–or–"she's not even trying to..."

At this point, it was pretty clear that the love they were sure could never fall down was pretty badly bruised. But after we agreed that naming and blaming the other couldn't possibly be the answer they needed to restore their lost love, things started to change. Their faces softened, the edge came off their accusations and their voices. Something had shifted. And then, as if suddenly tuned to the same wavelength, one of them asked a question that helped turn everything around, not just in our conversation but also in the way they had been looking at each other as the one to blame for their lost love. She was the one who spoke first:

"A few months ago there was nothing, no power in the universe, great enough to keep us apart, and now..."

He picked up her train of thought, as if they were one: "...and now the smallest thing comes between us, keeping us from being together."

I looked at the two of them sitting there, their hearts in hand, and my silence must have provoked the real question they had in mind when they asked to speak with me. She finished their thought:

"Surely there's some unseen force at work here, coming between us and doing its best to break us apart. Whatever you can do to help us get through this rough patch would really be appreciated"—and then, looking over at her fiancé, she finished her thought—"by both of us."

"All right then," I answered, "but I need to know, before we begin here, what is it the two of you are looking for here? Do you just want to get through this difference between you, or do you want to understand the *real* reason for it?"

My question seemed to surprise them both, but their answer came back to me in almost a single voice: "We want to understand..."

"Great...let's see what we can learn together, shall we? To start with, let me ask you a question; it may not make much sense at first, but your patience with sorting out the right answer to it will instruct both of you in some of the secrets of real relationship magic." And so I asked:

"When a great wind moves through the branches of a tree, making it sway and rock, left and right, has it come to knock the tree down? Or is that wind nature's way of secretly working to strengthen the roots of that tree? Which do you think is most true?"

It was he who spoke first. His answer sounded more like a question, but I could tell he had caught the meaning of what I had asked: "Well...I suppose it's come to strengthen the root system; at least...that seems to make the most sense."

"Yes, that's right; and so it can be with these clashes between the two of you. Much like a great wind, they can serve one of two purposes: they can either knock your love down and break it apart, or these same differences can be used to help you realize—and share in—a higher kind of love stronger than anything that seems to come between you. Which is it to be?"

They looked at each other, and then turned back to look at me:

"Please tell us what we need to know to stay together. How can we make our love grow stronger than any of our differences?"

Revelation #3: Awaken the Power to Start Solving All Your Relationship Problems

The knock at the front door took him by surprise. The sun was nearly down, and no one was expected. A moment later, brushing aside his resistance to leaving the comfort of his favorite living room chair—not to mention that he was about to miss a critical moment in his favorite TV series—he walked over to the door. For safety's sake, he put his eye up to the peephole to see who it might be.

He blinked a few times in disbelief: it was his eldest son, Aaron, standing on the other side of the door.

"What on earth," he thought to himself. In a heartbeat, he couldn't help but feel a cocktail of mixed emotions run right through him. After all, it's hard to be half happy and half angry at the same time. But, there it was. On one hand, he was glad, relieved actually, to see his boy. But, on the other hand, he could still feel the heat of the argument they had the last time they were together, and that was well over three years ago.

The blow-up between them happened right after Aaron's second marriage came apart at the seams. Aaron had come to see him, seeking solace. Being a good father, he wanted to share some of the hard-won understanding he'd gained over the forty-plus years of his marriage to Aaron's mother. Given the circumstances, he felt it was the right time to share some of the things he'd seen about his own character; certain stumbling blocks common to human nature that he knew his son was still blind to in himself.

But Aaron would have nothing to do with anything that even hinted he might be responsible for the misery that spoiled yet another relationship. The last words spoken between them were Aaron's:

"You don't know what you're talking about."

And with that, he walked out of the house, slamming the door behind him. But now, he was back. Had there been another tragedy in his son's life? There was only one way to find out... and so he opened the door, saying:

"Hello, son."

"Hi, Dad."

An awkward silence followed until, with a bit of a hesitation in his voice, Aaron spoke again: "Mind if... would it be okay if I came in for a moment...?"

Although somewhat shaken by this turn of events, his father said, "Why... no, I mean... yes! Of course, son; come in. What's on your mind?"

Over the course of the next hour, in fits and spurts, Aaron more or less confessed that over the last three years he'd been on a soul-searching mission, seeking the kind of knowledge he now suspected he'd turned his back on when he walked away that day. His pain and regret were evident; and he admitted—in spite of an additional trio of failed love interests—that he still didn't know what it takes to sustain a meaningful relationship. Near the end of their conversation, he said:

"Dad, I guess what I've come to ask—besides wanting to say I'm sorry for being a real ass—is *what am I missing here*? I mean, just when I think I've seen it all, that I've finally figured it all out, I run right into another wall. How am I ever going to find the kind of love that you and mom shared through all of your years together? And let's not kid ourselves... I know the two of you weathered some pretty tough times. And yet... your love remained."

After taking a long, piercing look into his son's eyes, and seeing the sincerity behind his question, he took a deep breath and answered:

"Well, you're right about one thing: you *are* missing a critical piece of understanding; it's what I intended to tell you before you turned your back on me. So, let's use this time we have together to make the very most of it that we can. Agreed?"

"Sure…that's why I'm here."

"First, there's something we must be clear about. You're mistaken if you believe—as you just said you do—that you've 'seen it all.' There's a crucial element that you're *not* seeing; one that I strongly suspect you've never even considered."

Then he took a measured breath and asked, deliberately: "Do you want me to go on?"

Aaron could tell by the tone of his father's voice, the way he expressed the question, that whatever was coming next wasn't going to be easy on him. But his longing to know the truth of his situation far outweighed any fear of hearing about the same. And so, trying not to sound as defensive as he was starting to feel, he answered:

"Yes…Dad; I do."

"This may be difficult to hear at first, son. And just so you know, I was equally clueless back in the day. But your mom helped me to see what I couldn't…just as I'm trying to do for you."

And then, obviously choosing his next few words carefully, he finished the thought he'd been leading up to all along:

"*What you have yet to see is the truth about … yourself.*"

And with that, Aaron took a deep breath, letting it out slowly, slightly nodding his head in agreement.

"I'd like to tell you how wrong you are, but … we both know it's true."

"Look, son, I know it feels a lot like you're at the 'end' of your rope, but it's not true; where you really are … is at the beginning … of something altogether new *in you*, and for all those you care about. But you have to be willing to see the truth of the way things are.

"Real lessons in self-knowledge are bitter to swallow, but they heal. In this instance, as you learn how to see yourself as you are, not only will you get to the root of your relationship problems … but this same discovery will also resolve them at the same time."

He paused for a moment, wondering if the meaning of his words had struck home; the slight smile on his son's face assured him it did, so he asked:

"Do you understand what I'm trying to tell you?"

"I think I get it, but I have some questions, if that's alright with you?"

"Son, nothing could make me happier than to share what I've learned with you. There's so much to see, and I have a good idea where we should start."

The Beauty of Balancing
the Relationship Equation

We all love to be loved; nothing is more gratifying, soul satisfying, than to feel as if someone cares for us. But true love is not just embracing those who want to embrace us in that same moment. Here's the rule:

Any form of one-sided love is destined to collapse under the weight of its own unstable foundation.

Hidden in this last insight, assuming we can muster the courage to take a deep look at its meaning, is the reason why so many of our relationships fail, or may be on the verge of falling down.

For any relationship to endure, let alone stand up to—and grow through—the appearance of the inevitable differences between two people, *it must have two sides to it.* While this last idea may seem obvious, don't let its simplicity fool you. As we're about to see, there's more than meets the eye here, and even more at stake.

The fact is that most of our relationships, even with those we love the most, are … *one-sided.*

I can almost hear the reader saying, "Yes, that's *exactly* what I've been trying to tell my partner, but he or she just doesn't get it!"

But we must be careful not to "rush to judgment." There's little doubt most of us already feel this way; whenever anyone fails to live up to our expectations, we stand ready to point the finger of blame. It is our partner, our friend, who is guilty of being "one-sided."

In our view, it's clear: that person is either unable or unwilling to see *our side* of the situation. And, just for the record, yes, this is likely true; in fact, odds favor that they are as blind to being "one-sided" as we are. But let's get to the real point here:

Our partner—whatever role he plays in our life, or however she may play it out—*is only half of the actual relationship equation*. And, just to be super clear, they are not even the most important half of this calculation. Here's why, and I trust you'll take the time you need to let the following truth sink in:

Love, the higher kind of love that matters most, *is not— cannot be—determined by what others do, or don't do, toward us*. This should be evident; after all, what kind of love is it that gives itself only to those who give it back when, and as, expected? Besides, if there's one thing we should all know by now it's this: it has *never* been in our power to make others love us as we would have them do.

We can't make someone be caring, or kind. No tender touch, no act of kindness or compassion can be coerced from someone we love, any more than we can force a rose to open her petals. Let our meaning here be clear: whenever we become negative toward others for not being as we want them to be toward us, blaming them for not being "loving" as expected, we are being *as one-sided* as they are, *whatever he or she may have done to make us feel that way.*

As challenging as it may be to our familiar ideas about who's at fault in the midst of some relationship meltdown—right when it feels as if our relationship is in a free fall—we must learn to ask ourselves the single most important question of all:

Who is responsible for that painful sense of difference that we feel *between our partner and ourself, whatever it may be that we point to in that moment?* Or, for that matter, who is responsible for the difference we feel between ourselves and anyone else, whether at work, in our family, or passing by on the street? A few routine examples will bring these last ideas into sharper focus.

Did that man—the disinterested teller who serves us at the bank, the distracted attendant waiting by our car window at the gas station—did he create that uneasy sense of difference between us as we do our business together?

Has that well-dressed woman in line ahead of us at the department store—buying an armful of expensive clothes—done anything to make us judge her as she spends—in ten minutes—what may take us a month to earn?

The answer to both questions above is…"No." Now, let's learn why this is true.

The majority of our experience with any person is pretty much just *one side* of that relationship and, to the point—it's *our* side of it. It's vital we see the fact of this last observation. After all, what is the nature—the actual "texture"—of our experience in any interaction, with anyone, if not *our feeling* about him or her in that same moment? Lastly, add to this equation the fact that *others see and experience us from their side of the aisle—as we do them*—and we can begin to see why no one ever wins such a fight!

The reality is that each and all of our relationships stir in us a host of strong feelings that, prior to their being stirred and awakened in us, we had no idea lay sleeping in our consciousness. These emotions range from deep delight to darkly disturbing, but to strengthen the main point: whatever someone awakens in us is…*our feeling*. Which brings us to the next three important points. The more you're able to see how they are secretly connected, the stronger will become your connection to a new order of love that can't be shattered by any storm.

1. Everyone in our life has a definite role to play in how we experience ourselves each moment; that's their part, as much as it is ours to play a similar role in their life. However, *they are not responsible for our negative reaction to what we see in ourselves when we're in their company.*

2. On the other hand, this isn't to say that we're to excuse others for their misguided treatment of us; only that *it's not our job to make anyone else see where he or she is "wrong."* Which leads us to the last of the three points.

3. If our wish is to discover a new and higher kind of love—the only one that can empower us to transcend our differences with our partner—then *we must begin to see our old excuses for finding fault with him or her as ... faulty!*

Let's review, and then summarize what we've learned up to this point in our study: when we look at someone, anyone, including those we love, through the eyes of some negative reaction, what is it that we're really looking at in that moment ... other than what *we don't want to see* standing there before us? The following explanation will help shed much-needed light on these last two all-important ideas:

1. *Negative reactions don't like anything!* Whatever gives them cause to be against someone or something, opposing life is what they like to "do."

2. While negative reactions are quick to look around for someone or something to blame in order to justify their painful presence within us, they are incapable of seeing—much like a skunk might look around and wonder, "What on earth is that stink!"—that *the*

suffering they hold others accountable for is really the result of being in their own dark company!

So, when our mind is filled with reasons for not liking someone—and our heart feels the same aversion, wishing to have nothing to do with whomever is considered in this way—the results are almost unavoidable: what else can we expect to see in our partner's eyes other than the same resentment or rejection they see flashing in our own? In other words, what they see in our eyes is our one-sided conclusion that they are to blame for our pain.

This insight should make it clear why, in the "heat" of a struggle with someone we care about, we see no love or understanding in their eyes. Why? Because they can't see any love or kindness in our own.

We want, actually secretly demand, whether they are family, friend, or loved one, that our partner not only understand what we're feeing, but why... and all without our having to tell them! We expect them to walk by our side, to see life through our eyes, and to support our mood swings with no questions asked. While we, for the most part, almost never consider what it's like to be on the other "side" of that relationship, looking at what our partner *sees in our eyes* that we can't, as yet, even see ourselves.

Until we can understand what those we love see—and feel—when they're with us, and vice-versa, of course—we are in a one-sided relationship headed for a rocky shore!

Put Yourself Into Your Partner's Shoes

There's a very well-known old proverb, the earliest traces of its familiar iteration dating back to the Cherokee tribe of Native Americans, that cautioned: *"Don't judge a man until you have walked a mile in his moccasins."*

Noted American author Harper Lee rewrote this same idea in her classic book, which was made into the film starring Gregory Peck, *To Kill A Mockingbird*: *"You never really know a man until you understand things from his point of view, until you climb into his skin and walk around in it."*

I think we can all agree that the heart and soul of this explicit wisdom goes back to an even older time, thousands of years ago, when Christ said to the masses gathered there for his Sermon on the Mount: *"All things whatsoever ye would that men should do to you, do ye even so to them."*[4]

Surely we can all see the good in this timeless principle. It has appeared, in one form or another, throughout the ages, and in many diverse places around the world.

Before Christ's instruction, Mosaic Law commanded: *"Whatever is hurtful to you, do not do to any other person."*[5]

Buddha guided his monks: *"Hurt not others with that which pains yourself."*[6]

---

4. Matthew 7:12, *The Holy Bible*, King James version.

5. Mosaic Law, Torah/Talmud.

6. *Udanavarga* 5.8.

Confucius taught: "*What you do not want done to yourself, do not do to others.*"[7]

None would disagree that this ideal codifies the foundation of human kindness. So, the real question before us is...how do we embody this living principle, especially in the midst of a disagreement with a loved one, right when we're sure our partner is "wrong"?

The following may be simple to say, but let me assure you little in this life is more difficult to do: *Before* we can know what it's like to "walk a mile in the moccasins" of our partner, *we must be willing to put ourselves into his or her shoes!*

In other words, we must agree—right in the midst of whatever may be the difference between us—to try and *see ourselves through* their *eyes.*

This *doesn't* mean we try to *imagine* what it's like for them to be in our company, or that we pretend to see their side so as to effect some temporary "peace." That would be spiritually dishonest, the opposite of what we want to be. Rather, we must make a new and honest kind of effort—through a deliberate shift in our perception—to see, to feel as best we can, what kind of energy we are expressing in that same moment.

In this way, not only do we get a glimpse of what our partner is seeing before his or her eyes, but also how one-sided we were when, the moment before we actually made

---

7. *The Analects of Confucius.*

this kind of shift in our attention, all *we were able to see* was someone to blame for how we feel.

Given the power to choose between the two possibilities outlined above, which of them do you think sounds most promising? To fight with our partner, and then make up—again and again—until all we have left to share are the cold remains of some unresolved pain...

...Or that we learn how to turn this kind of unpleasant encounter into a whole new kind of understanding, one that both illuminates *and* disarms the difference between our partner and ourself *before* it can escalate into a painful disagreement that no one wins?

We're on the verge of discovering one of the great secrets of relationship magic; we're about to learn how to align ourselves with a higher kind of love that will *always* work for us...regardless of whether our partner wants to be a part of the magic it makes...or not!

Helpful Questions and Answers

Question: I don't get it! Honestly, how can a better understanding of myself keep me from having the negative reaction I do every time I see my husband do something stupid, especially this one behavior that literally drives me up a wall?

Answer: The next time you want to jump on your husband for his misstep, try this: instead of unconsciously remembering all the reasons you have for opposing him in that moment, do your level best to remember where and how *you* have missed the mark in a similar way. Consciously choosing to recollect your similarity (with your partner's characteristic) not only disarms the part of yourself about to pounce upon it, but this level of self-honesty also dispels the illusion of difference imagined between the two of you, replacing it with a compassionate consideration born of wisdom and love.

Question: I hope you can help me understand why I feel so powerless when it comes to letting go of a particular old resentment I hold for my partner. On one hand, I want to drop it because I know it's no good for either of us; but no matter how much I try...I just can't seem to do it. What on earth is going on?

Answer: Given the honesty with which you've asked your question, see if the following insight doesn't shed some helpful light on your situation: the real problem isn't that there aren't right parts of you that want to let go of this grudge; it's obvious you can see the need to make this change. But what you have yet to see, and must if you would be free of this negativity, is that—at least for now—most of you *doesn't want to let it go.* The more clearly you come to see this shocking fact—how our lower nature loves to point out in others the very thing it says it can't stand to see—the sooner you will have the strength you need to succeed in letting go ... of both this bitterness and the unconscious nature that clings to it so tenaciously.

KEY LESSONS

1. Most people pounce on others as they do—when they do—not because they want to cause pain, but because they're afraid of being hurt. To see this truth is to realize that the real enemy of relationship is fear itself; for this dark state that dwells in the unenlightened heart knows that the best way to protect itself is by being "first" to find fault with another.

2. There can only be one reason why we become emotionally negative with our partner, let alone consent to identify with its dark and debilitating embrace: we've forgotten that in every moment we have a choice as to what we love, and whose company we keep, accordingly.

3. Any part of us ... any thought or feeling that pushes us to express—or otherwise say out loud these words to our partner—"See, I was right!" ... is wrong for (both of) us.

4

Start Taking Full Responsibility For Your Relationship

I hinted earlier at some of the new ideas about to follow, but a quick review of them will help speed our steps into this next part of our study.

Recall how we learned that the real reason, the unseen source of our negative reactions toward others, isn't necessarily what they do or don't do toward us; rather, we saw that most of our sense of resentment or disappointment with others—the real source of that "thorn" in our side—is some invisible demand of ours that goes before us into all of our relationships.

These impossible expectations—placed on friends, family, and our loved one—are such that none can possibly live up to their mandate. And, much to the point, it's not just people we know who have this power to trouble us at the push of the proverbial "button."

For example, have you ever been sitting in a coffee shop, or waiting in your car at a red light, when you looked up for a moment to see someone who instantly "bothers" you? Maybe it's the way some man is walking with his chin stuck out, announcing the chip he has on his shoulder; perhaps it's the way she "tosses" her head, flinging her hair to one side, obviously acting nonchalant? How about this familiar scene: you go to a dinner party and sit across from someone you've never met. And, before you're even introduced, it's clear that you don't like him or her one bit! Here's the explanation of this kind of negative reaction that we can have at the drop of a hat:

Our studies have revealed that each of us has a special role to play in the grand scheme of creation. We've seen that timeless forces of every possible character never stop "touching" us, literally weaving their way in and out of our being in every passing moment. This makes us a partner in the "cosmic dance" of yin and yang, an instrument of constantly shifting active and passive energies, so that in one moment we may feel attracted to someone, wanting to know him or her better... and, after only a moment of being near to them, our only wish is to get away!

This means that even as we're receiving these celestial forces into us, we're also radiating them at the same time. Let's take a moment here to consider this last important idea. For one thing, it means not only are we, ourselves, directly involved in the constant interaction of these unseen forces within us, but they *have their "own" relationship* as well, whose effects we know very little about.

Nevertheless, our experience of their interaction can be thought of as one of those sudden feelings that come over us—"for no reason." We call these unpredictable emotional energies being in a "mood."

The question before us now—given our discoveries—is this: do our relationships have to be defined by the interaction of these interior forces playing themselves out in the dark of us? Must we be "pushed" into a fight with our partner, with anyone, just because we feel the presence of some pressure in us "telling" us that he or she is responsible for our stress? The answer is no.

The Power to Choose the Relationship You Really Want

The new insights we've gained into our present relationship with celestial forces—whose ceaseless interactions have a direct bearing on how we see and experience all of our relationships in life—lead us to this next very important point: *these forces are blind*; of themselves, they know nothing of their own nature; they cannot see the kind of experiences they create through their interactions; and *neither is their individual character capable of caring about any of the above.*

And yet, even though these forces are blind—and perhaps, under their influence, we may have acted equally so—all of this can change because of this one remarkable fact that follows: *we can learn to see them.* Not only can we become aware of these unseeing forces as they play out their designated role in us but, by the same light of this awareness, we will be given authority over them! Let's look at a "real-time" example of how this kind of higher consciousness might work to put us in charge of any challenging relationship.

Imagine for a moment that you're standing in line to pay for your groceries. The next thing you know, a large man steps right on your sore toe! Up come waves of negative energy accompanied by a host of justifiably angry thoughts ready to lash out at this most inconsiderate person. But then, just as you're about to lash out in pain, you see something about him that instantly changes everything you were about to do: he's carrying a red-tipped cane. It's obvious: he's visually impaired, which means...he did not mean to hurt you; he just couldn't see what he was doing.

Your sudden realization doesn't make the pain in your toe go away, but it does make it possible for you to see through, and then let go of, what was, a moment before, an irrational, blame-fueled reaction. Why? Because *you* can see both sides of the story in that same moment. This new and higher kind of awareness of the whole situation is the same as being empowered to see, and then make, the right kind of choice for both of you. Now, let's illustrate how this last example might play out in "real time" when it feels as if someone is out to hurt you. As hard as this may be to believe—for the time being anyway—*no one is trying to "step on your toes."*

I can almost hear you say: "Now...wait just a moment; you don't understand how my partner treats me, or how my supervisor or coworkers can't wait to criticize me, deliberately crushing my hopes."

Listen: we're not saying that people aren't cruel, or that unkind behavior is supposed to be overlooked or, worse, accepted as the cost of that relationship. Doing so would be as much a mistake on our part as others are mistaken when listening to their pain tell them who to blame for it. But are these the only two choices possible when one of our relationships turns painful: lash back, or accept the lashing?

Experience proves that neither of these choices ever brings about a positive change in our relations with others, but at last we're learning why this is true: *these choices are not made by us*; they are made *for us* anytime we say "I" to that immediate resistance we feel whenever someone, *anyone*, opposes our wishes. Now, let's look at these last few ideas by looking into a real example of what is most likely a fairly common experience of ours.

Can you think of any disagreement between two people that doesn't start with something like: "*I want what I want!*" And how, when what we want doesn't line up with what our partner wants, the battle lines are drawn. And that's just the beginning! Depending on which of us initiates the encounter, the other is left with but one of two basic choices: agree and give in to our partner's demand so that there's no dispute left to resolve and life can just move on, or—as is usually the case—one of us disagrees, and tensions mount.

As things heat up, as they must whenever differing wills collide, the only thing we can see in these moments is what's wrong with our partner; each of us opposes the other for the same reason. But the unseen story here, the real driving force behind our dispute, is that *both of us are momentarily blind*; our agitated state of mind sees only who's to blame for its pain, which is the same as seeing only "our" side of story.

Use the Light of This Insight to End Any Fight

Now let's look at these same principles from a slightly different point of view. When we struggle with someone, as holds true in any "wrestling" match, each of us wants to come out "on top!" But here's the rub: whenever we look for a way to be more "powerful" than our partner, all we do is secretly strengthen the exact same wish in him or her; and we all know *that* drill, where what starts out as a plain old "tit for tat" disagreement soon turns into a painful knock-down, drag-out fight.

Which brings us to the main point of this part of our study: it's *not* more power that we need; what we really need is to *stop agreeing to make ourselves powerless*. Let's spend a moment or two looking at this last unusual idea. It will help us to better see what happens to us whenever we look at our partner through the "eyes" of one of these blind forces.

When in a fight of any kind, over anything, we look over at our partner and "see"—almost magically—exactly what's wrong with him or her in that moment. So confident are we in our conclusion as to the nature of *their* problem that the following has almost no chance to dawn on us:

We can't see that our partner is looking at us in this exact same kind of "light"... that is not a light at all. *Negative reactions have no awareness of themselves*; there is *no* light in them, any more than a cluster of bombs has compassion for whatever they fall on and destroy.

What we need in these moments is *the light of a new kind of understanding.* We need to awaken to, and realize, a higher level of awareness that allows us to appreciate two things at once: first, to see that just like us, our partner is in some kind of pain and is being moved, just as we are, to find someone to blame for it. In other words, *the same negative forces are at work in both of us.* And second, even though these opposing forces are blind, *that doesn't mean that we have to be!* The more we can wake up to the presence of these unconscious forces and how, undetected, they keep us at odds with one another, the freer we become to love without their limitations.

Let's summarize our discoveries so far: when we're negative—in a "power struggle" with our partner over whatever is being contested—we're reduced to being little more than a puppet. We're literally "strung out"—momentarily animated—by unseeing forces within us that can only do one thing: *mechanically oppose whatever seems to oppose them.*

I understand this last image is not very flattering, but let's be honest: experience validates the fact of it. Each time we're drawn into a fight, it's exactly as if someone "turns out the lights." All we can "see" in that slowly enveloping darkness of our negative state is someone that we're sure it's our duty to change, control, or "make sorry" for what he or she has done to us... *even as they are trying to do the same to us.*

The conflict in these emotional tugs-of-wars is the stuff of sorrow, and take us nowhere except back and forth. If this is true, and we know it is, then with what are we left? From where will come this new light needed in the midst of these dark moments knowing, as is obvious by now, that *we can't illuminate our partner?*

Assuming we can all agree with this last revelation—that it's not in our power to illuminate our partner—here's what we're left with; its simplicity is both beautiful and powerful at the same time:

If we hope to see any real transformation take place in our relationships—whether with family, friends, or our partner for life—*then it is we who must become illuminated.*

The kindness, the patience, the love we seek is *going to have to start with us*... even if our partner throws our best efforts right back in our face!

Challenging? No doubt—perhaps more so than anything we may have ever tried to do before. Rewarding? Let's see, and then *you* decide:

What if rather than allowing these blind opposing forces to set you against your partner, *you could learn how to start using them*; where even a hint of their pressure would not only awaken you to their presence but—in that same moment—empower you to consciously separate yourself from their punishing influences? This would be like owning a kind of spiritual "alarm clock" that goes off just before you start to blame—or resent—your partner; a silent but unmistakable alert system that serves, at once, to reveal and release you from the unseen parts of your own consciousness that tend to automatically oppose any unwanted moment.

Meet the "Intensively Caring" You

We can summarize all that we've learned so far in the form of a special exercise. However, it turns out that the best way to convey this closing lesson requires a little play on words, the purpose of which I trust will soon become clear.

Most of us have heard of an area in a hospital called "ICU." These three letters are an acronym that is an abbreviation for "Intensive Care Unit."

The ICU is a designated floor in a hospital where, due to a severe injury or sudden onset of a life-threatening health issue, one is taken to receive round-the-clock attention. Even if we've never been in such a place, it's likely we know someone who has.

Now, keeping this same idea in mind, although this is obviously far less dramatic: what happens after a "traumatic" day at the office or at home with a pile of mounting bills? Even an unexpected run-in with a friend can deliver a crushing blow, leaving us feeling battered and broken. Following a "hard landing" of any such kind...do we not look to our partner to "intensively care" for us? Of course we do. When we hurt we want to be consoled, comforted; and barring that, at least allowed to blow off some of the steam that's been building up in us.

Now, as a rule, we're not aware of these unspoken demands...that is, not until our partner fails to give us the attention we expect. In those moments, we perceive their inability to give us the intensive care we feel we deserve as indifference to our pain. But the following insight makes it clear that our view of that moment is not the whole story. After all, our partner—likely having had a few "pile-ups" of his or her own that day—is also looking to us for the same kind of "intensive care." And there you have it: *a standoff*, where each party involved—failing to feel properly cared for, as deserved—sees the other as being insensitive!

If we want to end this kind of endless "blame game," then one of us has to step up and begin seeing through the unconscious forces that drive this wheel of misfortune.

The moment we feel the onset of any disagreement with our partner we must agree to be a kind of "torch bearer." In other words, *we* must be the one who understands that the only reason we're about to "go another round" is because *we're both momentarily blind*, meaning *all* we can see is our partner as the cause of the discomfort we feel.

Being able to understand the reality of our situation is the same as being empowered to act toward it in a completely new way. If we can see that the real cause of our mounting conflict is due to this kind of blindness, then the healing prescription is right in front of our eyes. Which brings us to the little play on words that I mentioned at the start of this chapter section.

Instead of allowing ourselves to be drawn into that unconscious game of "tug-of-war" over who cares, and who doesn't—where all we see before us is someone denying us the "intensive care" we feel we deserve—we use our awareness of this struggle between opposing forces *to let go of the rope* and do something entirely new:

We practice "ISM." Three letters that stand for three simple words: *"I see myself."*

As we're about to discover, this little phrase, *"I see myself,"* describes a single action that has the power to change the heart of whoever is willing to embrace its practice. But, before we examine this exercise, let's take a closer look at what it means to "see ourselves"—*as we are*—especially when our partner has failed to please us.

To begin with, it's impossible to see ourselves—as *we* are—when all we can see before us is someone else who's to blame for a feeling that we don't want. The truth is, at least for now, we can't see anything at all about ourselves when we're in the heat of a disagreement with anyone, even if it is with someone we love.

We can't see our own flashing eyes, because all they're capable of looking at is who to blame for the heat rising up behind them.

We don't hear the defiant tone in our voice, because it's being drowned out by the voices in our head, justifying our right to be angry, disappointed, resentful, or otherwise upset.

And we've almost no sense at all of these mounting pressures in us, because we've been rendered numb by the drumming of these unconscious forces as they seek, and always seem to find—*in our partner*—a reason for being so disturbed.

Learn to See Yourself
Through the Eyes of the One You Love

To see the truth of the above is to understand how important it is for us to be as *fully mindful* as possible in the midst of a disagreement with our partner. We need to be completely present to whatever is coming up and out of us—not only aware of the kind of thoughts and feelings coursing through us, but equally sensitive to the kind of energy we can intuit is accountable for their appearance.

Now, let's see why our willingness to enter into this healing space called "ISM" empowers us—on the spot—to realize the possibility of a whole new and higher relationship with our partner, starting with this:

Seeing myself as I am allows me *to see what* you're *looking at, at the same time!*

Let me rephrase this same idea in another way to give us a slightly different slant on it. When was the last time, in the middle of a fight with anyone, you came to a stop and silently, deliberately asked yourself this question: "I wonder what it's like for you to be experiencing me, *as I am*, right now?"

You might be thinking, "Why on earth would I ever want to know such a thing?"

Because until we can see what we're actually "giving" our partner in a conflicted moment with them, we'll never understand why they often feel as if they're being punished by our presence. But now let's look behind the "curtain" during these encounters and see what we're "giving" our partner that makes them want to push us away.

Outwardly we may be working to exhibit a warm, caring appearance, but inwardly we are in a controlled "burn."

Outwardly we may be ever so careful with the words we use, trying to convey a sense of patience, a willingness to understand, but inwardly we are at the end of our rope.

In either case, one thing should be clear: while we're identified with the positive role we're playing, feeling pleased to see ourselves in the light of the part we're acting out, our partner is definitely *not* seeing us as we've imagined ourselves to be. What they're experiencing in that moment is a negative energy radiating out of us that can't be disguised. And, as it pours over them, it makes them want to push back against it! In this scenario the only thing that changes is who's pushing and who's being shoved...that is, until these roles naturally reverse themselves as a matter of course.

The point being, nothing can change between us as long as we're both clinging to a position *that doesn't even exist* without what it unconsciously opposes in our partner.

Your willingness to ponder the next two questions will help shed some valuable light on this last insight:

Does my disappointment with you exist without whatever it is that I expect from you? (Hint: Of course not!)

Can any resentment I feel for you failing to sing my praises come into play without my having first imagined myself as worthy of being exalted?

It should be clear: *Whatever we find offensive about our partner only punishes us—in the unique manner that it does—because it strikes something unique within us that's waiting to be offended!*

This explains why, if we want an open and healthy relationship with our partner, we must do the interior work of practicing "ISM." The conscious choice to *see ourselves as we are* in the midst of any struggle with our partner *changes us* and, in turn, everything about that moment.

But let's not minimize the difficulty of working to consciously see ourselves as we are, especially when there's been a run-in with our partner.

The whole notion of "ISM" feels warm and fuzzy to imagine... that is, *until* our partner challenges our view of how things are supposed to be; so that when the time comes to see ourselves as we are—versus trying to change what we see as "objectionable" in our partner—odds favor we'll fall back into the familiar "blame game." And that's okay; not to worry. Here's why:

Being able to observe even the smallest of your own negative reactions, and to recognize on the spot that *it— that opposing force—is not you*, means that a whole new level of awareness is now awake in you. The light of this higher self-awareness, now united with your willingness to see yourself—as you are—has done the unthinkable: it has set you free... *from yourself.* For the first time, you're able to step outside the negative influence of these unconscious forces, making it possible to love your partner as you've always wanted to: unconditionally.

We must not wait to start our practice; the truth is that every moment is the right moment to see ourselves as we are…regardless of whoever may be our "partner" of the moment.

Maybe it's the person in that long line with us, complaining about how slowly things are moving. There's no better time to practice "ISM" than when some part of yourself can't wait to "pounce" on the impatience of someone else. How about being stuck behind a driver on the freeway who won't speed up or get out of the way? Practice "ISM" and "arrest" that part of yourself that's always rushing somewhere, resisting everyone and anything in its way!

The more places we employ this interior practice, the sooner we will find ourselves living from a higher level of Self that cannot be made to turn against anyone, let alone the one we love. You've heard the expression "Practice makes perfect." Seeing ourselves as we are *is love in action* because it's the same as consciously illuminating those lower, unconscious levels of self that stand in the way of all that is kind, caring, and compassionate.

Speaking of illuminating these lower levels of self that are incapable of love, here's one last insight whose importance can't be overstated.

This unconscious nature—and its opposing forces that serve to keep us at odds with one another—*does not* want to be brought into the light of higher self-awareness that comes with seeing ourselves as we are. It lives in the dark of us, and wants to keep it that way. To that end, and to ensure that no sustained light reaches into its lair to reveal its covert operations, here's one of its favorite ways of protecting itself: anytime we catch even a fleeting glimpse of its dark character—it immediately tries to turn the tables on us by inciting us to judge ourselves for what we see!

Most of us have some knowledge of that timeless teaching, "*Judge not, that ye be not judged.*"[8] Now we know something of its inner meaning: *being deceived into judging ourselves for whatever shadows we see hiding within us is how these in-the-dark parts keep themselves out of the light, and out of our sight.* Here's the only thing you need to know to disarm this deceptive nature: *there is no such thing as a bad fact about yourself.* Anything that wants you to believe otherwise, or that tries to punish you for what you've been given to see, is desperate to get you to look the other way!

Helpful Questions and Answers

Question: My husband does things that make me so angry. Are you saying it's wrong for me to step up and to speak my mind about how I feel?

Answer: Of course not: it may seem subtle, but there's a big difference between bringing up an issue, some concern

---

8. Matthew 7:1. *The Holy Bible*, King James version.

you have with your partner, and striking back at them in pain over what you would blame them for. In other words, it's not so much *what* you say, but "*who*"—what part of you—starts talking for you in that moment. Here's one good way to ensure that you choose the right time for engaging your partner over any problem brewing between the two of you: wait, patiently—even if it takes twenty-four hours—until whatever part of you that feels compelled to blame, or that wants to complain, subsides. By following these instructions, you'll be aware of your negative state, instead of acting as its unconscious instrument.

Question: My wife has a real problem with anger; honestly, I think she likes to fight! Try as I may to stay detached, she always manages to drag me into an argument with her…and I mean we can argue over nothing! What can I do? How can I get her to see what she's doing to our relationship?

Answer: Blaming someone else's anger for our inability to remain above and untouched by its negative influence is like resenting a rain cloud for getting us wet when we walk outside and into its downpour. The only thing that can drag us into a fight with our partner, regardless of what he or she wants to fight with us over, is an in-the-dark part of us that's secretly been waiting for a good fight. If you really want to stop fighting, and free both of you at the same time, then set the following intention, here and now, as if your life depends on it: *no matter what*, refuse to climb into the ring the next time she wants to rumble. The more you're able to observe these parts of yourself that are so easily enticed to fight, the clearer it will become who you can no longer afford to be. And once you're able to stay out of the ring, then who is left there for your wife to fight with? No longer having any opponent, she will be able to see—and hopefully set down—the same parts of herself that you did. Peace will fall onto your house.

KEY LESSONS

1. All of our relationships, particularly with those we love, exist for a single beautiful purpose that expresses itself in two different ways. First, our partner—whether spouse, that "special" someone, or even a would-be companion—is in our life to help us grow; to provide just the conditions we need to become that better, truer person that they see in us, just waiting to be brought forth. But the other and equally important half of this same purpose and promise—without which the first part can't be realized—is as follows: our partner is also there in our life to help us see *everything in us that now stands in the way* of our realizing this same higher possibility.

2. It feels as if our irritation over feeling emotionally slighted by our partner proves that we know the

right way that we ought to be treated by the same. But a closer look proves otherwise. If we really know what it means for someone to be caring, then why would we be so careless with ourselves as to hold on to a negative state that can't care for anything or anyone? *It doesn't even care for itself.*

3. No one, no event, is the sole "cause" of what we see as disturbing us, any more than a mirror is "responsible" for showing us something in it that we would rather not see!

5

The Secret of
Making a Fresh Start

Do you remember the first time you fell in love...or even sensed the possibility? In a heartbeat, you were awash in a flood of new feelings you didn't even know had been missing from your life! It was like stepping out of a monochrome world into a living rainbow whose "pot of gold" was just the way your partner looked at you, or touched you; where whatever might come "tomorrow" didn't matter as long as you could meet it together. You thought it would never end.

Then, as time passes, things seem to change; not all at once, of course, but in measured beats. His once adorable, quirky attitude toward money or your family becomes an irritant; her sly smile that used to delight you, knowing she was as clever as a fox, now seems to challenge your opinion on almost everything you have to say!

What's happened? Where did the love go?

Depending on which of these two parties you ask, their response may differ, but the outcome remains the same: little by little, some of the things that used to thrill us about our partner now send a little shiver down our spine. Patience with our partner's missteps turns to blaming them for stepping on toes already trod on, swollen, and sore to the slightest touch. And, as we've already discovered, the more we blame our partner for this kind of pain, the more they're moved to want to do the same; so that, under law, all that can change between us is the intensity of our opposition to one another.

We all know this kind of relationship warfare. Our partner tosses a cruel comment at us, or drops a "bombshell" of some false accusation. Feeling compelled to defend ourselves, we pick it up and hurl it back. The argument escalates, and the dark pattern reseeds itself again, fueled by a growing frustration because the only thing that can change in this game of "king of the mountain" is who gets to temporarily stand in the top spot!

Pull Yourself Out of This Common Relationship Trap

In a discussion with a small group of students, as we worked to better see and understand the futility of gaining an imagined "upper hand" in a war where both parties are victimized by the same misunderstanding, I asked them the following question:

"What difference is the outcome of any conflict with someone we love–'win' or 'lose'–when it changes *nothing about these unseen parts of us that live to oppose whoever seems to oppose them?*" The answer was fairly unanimous; if both parties feel the other is at fault for the conflict, nothing can change save for the escalating level of blame. Once that much was clear, I added the following comment: "No matter how convinced we are that it's in our partner's "best interest" that we point out some critical fault of theirs... of this we can be certain: the only thing *any* of these actions do to our relationship is make it worse."

Apparently what I said struck a note with one of the students there, sparking a question in her that, as she framed it, got everyone's attention. As she spoke about her current struggle with her partner, it was apparent–by how attentive everyone became listening to her story–that she wasn't the only one struggling to understand the topic at hand.

"I admit it would be foolish to question what you've described here. It's pretty much the pattern of what happens whenever I get into a fight with my long-time boyfriend." She paused for a moment, looked off in the distance as if seeing something there that called out for her attention. A moment later, she went on to describe what she had just seen:

"In truth, it seems strange now that I've never thought to discuss this with him, but it's a fair bet that neither of us feels good after an argument, regardless of which of us gets our way! And while I can't speak for him, I'm sure if he could choose a better path than blaming me for the pain he feels, that he would...as would I. But neither one of us can see the mess we're about to make of our relationship until it's too late." Again she paused, obviously concerned with what her own deliberations had helped her to formulate in the question that followed:

"What I guess I'm asking is...what, if anything, can we do...to break this pattern that I see now is starting to break us apart?"

The rest of this chapter section outlines, in detail, the answer to her question. It also provides helpful insights into how we can use any unwanted moment in our relationship to transform everything about it...including ourself, *and* our partner.

Imagine for a moment that you've gone for a walk through a countryside that was once dotted with homesteads. Here and there you can see the remnants of old foundations set in stones taken from the fields. With your attention captured by your imagination as it ponders what were simpler times and places, you trip over a small boulder you didn't see in your path.

The next thing you know, you're not only falling forward, but headlong you go into the mouth of a shrub-covered, hand-dug well. A moment later, after your head has popped up above the ice-cold water and you realize you're unharmed, panic sets in; you spin around in the water looking for a way out. But, regardless of the direction you turn, all you can see and touch are the slippery, moss-laden stone walls that surround you.

And then—as if an angel had whispered in your ear—you suddenly see the solution to your situation. You'd been looking in every direction but the right one; *you'd forgotten to remember to look up*. What a relief! Suspended there, just a foot above your head, is an old wooden bucket attached to a rope stretching down from above. You reach up, grab hold, and—none the worse for wear, save for being a little cold and embarrassed—you pull yourself out of the dark and into the sunlight.

The first part of the above analogy speaks pretty well to what happens to us when we "fall" into a fight with our partner. Maybe it's a knee-jerk reaction to being blamed for something; perhaps it's a negative reaction born of seeing something in our partner we feel can't go unopposed. The truth is...*there's no "right" side in any fight as long as we're walled in by some old negative reaction*. On the other hand, just above us—and easily within our reach in this same dark moment—is the new self-understanding we need to climb up and out of that fight.

In the heat of any pitched moment—surrounding and walling us in—is a strong, very familiar feeling that the only way to survive this conflict is to prevail over it; and so we act accordingly. But, under law—a celestial principle that governs all worlds—is the following truth: for every action we take, always comes an equal and opposite reaction.

Let's look at this principle in real time as it impacts a relationship between "Paul" and "Mary"—two people who love one another:

Paul feels Mary give him a "push" of some kind, i.e., blames, criticizes, or judges him in some way. Without thinking, Paul pushes back with what he feels he must to defend himself, given the undeserved attack. Mary instantly feels the pressure of his negative reaction that, in turn, gives her all the reasons she needs to feel validated for her original attack on his character. She doubles down, and round and down goes the relationship.

This is why the proverbial "push comes to shove" never goes anywhere: our unawareness of these opposing forces is the same as being a prisoner of the pattern they make in their struggle against one another. Which brings us to a great mystery: if no part of a painful pattern can ever change the pattern that it's a part of... then how can that pattern ever change? The following insight helps show us the way out:

Hoping to make a real change in some painful pattern with a loved one, without being willing to risk what may happen to you by deliberately stepping outside of that pat-

tern, is like walking around in a circle and wondering why you're not getting anywhere.

It's worth noting here that the brilliant physicist Albert Einstein reached the same conclusion as above, only using different words: "No problem can be solved from the same level of consciousness that created it."

Catch This Spark That Ignites the Fight Before It Becomes a Flame

Before we can learn how to step outside the pattern set into motion by some habitual negative reaction toward our partner, we need a better understanding of the underlying forces that create it. In other words, we must find a way to look at these same moments through a "new set of eyes." We'll dig a little deeper into this unusual idea in chapter 8, but the following insights will give us a good start.

Obviously, we can't change our "eyes" themselves; but what we can do is "see" that our experience of any given moment is very much connected to what we think we understand—or don't—about it. Here's a simple illustration to help enlarge and clarify this last important idea.

A child who doesn't understand the nature of a dark shadow that suddenly appears on her wall in the dead of night is instantly frightened by what she sees. In much the same way, when we see some "scary" characteristic appear in our partner, a quality whose nature we don't understand—but *think* we do—we react in a childish manner, and try to "make it go away!"

This insight helps explain why painful patterns in our relationships repeat themselves in the way they seem to do: each time an incident sparks a negative reaction in us, we've basically no choice but to "look" at it through the same level of misunderstanding that initiated the conflict in the first place.

You've heard the expression, "like throwing gasoline on a fire to put it out." Well, that's exactly what resisting our partner does each time he or she displeases us in some way. It doesn't put out the sparks that are flashing between the two of you. Instead it fans them until they burst into a flame that burns everyone involved.

If our real wish is to leave the blame game behind us, to walk away from that dreaded feeling like we constantly need to defend ourselves from the same, then the work ahead of us is clear: before we can leave these painful patterns behind us once and for all, we have to outgrow our present level of understanding that's secretly responsible for them.

Let's be clear: no one is saying it's easy to walk away from the painful patterns that run through our relationships, and that cause them to gradually unravel. However, given our recent discoveries, the following should be equally clear: until we understand the nature of these painful patterns—including the part of our lower nature responsible for their reappearance—we will remain shackled to them.

I understand that insights like this don't go down easy, but then again, neither does the medicine we sometimes have to swallow in order to heal. In fact, and much to the point, I remember a particular conversation I had with a middle-aged woman who—after hearing me say at a seminar that all painful patterns require two players—wanted to argue the point.

"Hold on just a moment, if you please. I like the idea of being able to drop an argument before a spark turns into a flame, but let's get real. It may be different for other couples, but there's so much old baggage between my partner and me, our fights are pre-packed! How can we possibly hope to overcome the past…given some of the harsh things we've said and done to one another?"

"That's just the point; the task before us isn't to 'overcome' whatever may have happened in the past. We can't change what has passed between us and our partner any more than lamenting over sour milk can make it taste sweet again."

"What am I missing here? If we don't overcome these differences between us, what's left? For instance, one of the ways we move past fighting with each other whenever some old conflict reappears is by agreeing to live with a kind of uneasy peace between us until things blow over; we reach an unstated compromise that seems to cool things off enough for us to move on."

"I know it's said that 'time heals all wounds,' but our experience with our partner proves that to be mostly untrue; what we call 'compromising' with our partner—for the most part—is an unconscious agreement to live with one kind of trouble in order to avoid a bigger one. But burying differences doesn't free us from their weight, and this level of solution soon festers, becoming a breeding ground of resentment carried forward.

"To this fault-ridden recipe, add the idea that struggling to overcome something that nags us about our partner amounts to trying to lift ourselves by our own bootstraps; it just can't be done. Here's why: how can we bring an end to what troubles us about a loved one when the real problem between us is *our* impossible-to-please expectations of them? Not to mention—more often than not—we don't even know what these demands are until something in their actions or character proves to disappoint us!"

"Then how am I to react when my husband sets me off? You can't be suggesting that I stand there and let him get away with it?"

"If we can start to see that we're at least 50 percent responsible for whatever we feel opposed to in our partner, then we should also be able to see why our negative reaction to him or her can never bring about any real solution. How can it...when these mechanical reactions are the unseen driving force behind whatever may be that painful pattern we hope to change? Wanting to change the out-come of disagreeable moments with a loved one, without changing what gets them started, is like trying to change your cold, wet clothes while standing outside in a thunderstorm."

As long we are in a relationship with someone, there must be differences between us; and these disparities are mandatory to our development. We've shown that were it not for the presence of these opposing forces, and what they reveal to us about ourselves, there would be no way for us to grow, to become more kind, compassionate, and loving partners. Here's the point:

It's *the differences between you and your partner* that help perfect *both* of you—not only as lovers and friends, but also as individuals. To acknowledge the truth of this insight and, at the same time, admit we are not yet able to act in accordance with it, places us right where we need to be in order to receive the higher self-knowledge that follows:

Before we can hope to shatter the pattern of familiar conflicts with our partner, we need a new level of under-standing to take with us into those same moments. This includes being willing to see that relying on our present level of understanding to solve our disputes is like asking the "fox to guard the henhouse."

After all, what are most arguments about between partners? You displease me, and then I let you know that I don't like it. Next moment, you're displeased with me for being disappointed with you. Now each of us tries to get the other to see where they're wrong, thereby proving that our understanding of the situation is the superior one! But let's be clear: there's nothing superior in this kind of suffering when all it guarantees is that we'll get to do it over again. Which begs the question: Why are we, as yet, unable to see the futility of fights like these? What has us so blinded that we can't see we're about to purchase another round trip ticket to nowhere? The following answer may be surprising, but the more we're able to understand it, the freer we will be from the unseen parts of ourself that are luring us into these unwanted patterns:

It is impossible to find ourselves in a drawn-out disagreement with a loved one without having first listened to our own negative reaction *tell us* why *it has to be that way.*

Of course, as we all know too well, this reaction, including its supporting cast and crew, takes center stage before we even know the show has started! But, with just the light of a little higher self-knowledge, we can peek behind the curtain of these unexpected moments and see how the stage gets set for our fall.

All relationship-wrecking reactions appear in the same moment as our partner's disapproving face or offhand comment. That certain look or tone of voice is all it takes. Each and all of these negative reactions "arrive" on the scene script in hand, reading off the entire history of why things are the way they are, and what's wrong with the person in question. Everything is wordlessly explained. It's all just there, including a set of suggested actions to take to make sure the situation doesn't get out of hand.

In other words, *our negative reactions come preloaded with the reason for their appearance.* But they are not to blame for how readily we accept what they tell us is real. Here's the real problem: we've yet to see how identifying with their misperception of the moment—that always includes who's to blame, and a plan to put things right—is like jumping onto a merry-go-round, hoping that if we ride on it long enough, we'll stop going around and around. Stepping out of this cycle requires we rise above the level of consciousness responsible for its continuation.

Learn This Lesson and Take the Limits Off Your Ability to Love

Now let's get started gathering the facts we need to release ourselves from any kind of painful relationship pattern *before* we have to go through it again.

Never mind whatever may be telling you that such a power doesn't exist. It does, and of this you may be assured: *love is not limited to* our *present view of what it can … or can't do!*

As contradictory as it may seem, our almost inescapable sense of being unable to rise above problem patterns with our partner resides in the last place any of us would ever think to look for it: *a false belief that we already understand the true nature of love*. A few simple examples will help prove this last point.

If our understanding of love includes the belief that loving someone means agreeing to live with a mounting resentment toward him or her, then what else can happen as a result of that idea other than always coming to another tipping point? A fight ensues, and the pattern starts over.

But real love, meaning a love that belongs to a higher level of being, keeps no record of wrongs.

This higher order of love is able to see and understand what we have yet to realize: our partner doesn't *want* to be mean or cruel, any more than we do. But all he or she knows to do with the onset of some pain is to lash out at whatever or whoever they understand as being at cause for their suffering. One partner feels angry, the other feels blamed; both are in pain, with neither one knowing the *real* cause of their unwanted situation.

If it's our present understanding of love that anytime our partner fails to please us, it means that he or she doesn't love us—at least, not as we imagine they should—then what happens to our love? It turns cold in less than a heartbeat! But higher love cannot be turned upside down and turn into its opposite, any more than a ray of light can be made into a shadow. Even when someone seems to be deliberately doing all he can to provoke a negative response, real love *never* punishes. Love never fails...to love.

With these last few thoughts in mind there should be little doubt that the limit of our present understanding about the true nature of love is not the same as the limit of its possibility; and if we even suspect this is true then it should lead us to ask ourselves the following question: how do we rise above this unseen limitation in our relationships, and where do we get started?

The good news is there's nothing we have "to do" in order to deepen the love we share with our partner; we only need to see that this higher order of love has *always* been within us, "hidden in plain sight." As we're about to see, and prove to ourselves, this last idea isn't nearly as mysterious as it sounds at first. Please welcome the following "eye-opening" explanation.

It's my hope that somewhere along the line in your past studies of spiritual ideas you ran across this old adage: "As above, so below." If not, no worries; this timeless teaching comes to us through a fragment of writing found on the Emerald Tablet of Hermes Trismegistus. Ancient myth has it that this secret celestial principle was whispered to Hermes Trismegistus, that—in turn—he might help humanity awaken to see, and realize, the existence of a living relationship between the imperceptible laws of heaven and their physical expression on earth.

In other words, all that we're given to see—and that we go through with our partner—is actually a physical manifestation of the invisible principles that give rise to that experience.

To date—and much to the point of this book—ours has been pretty much a one-sided affair with those we love because our relationship with them is governed by unseen forces that determine how we interact with them. But our growing awareness of these unconscious reactions, including the thoughts and feelings that serve to support their appearance, changes everything. Before, we were more like pawns in the hands of these celestial powers that we could neither see, nor understand. Now we're going to learn how to be their partner... with a majority interest!

Let's look into a common experience to catch a glimpse of where and how these unseen celestial principles express themselves in the middle of usual social affairs. We'll derive the most benefit from the following illustration by remaining mindful of this next special key lesson:

Awareness of any negative reaction that comes up within us, or in our partner, is more than just a window into our unconscious nature whose untamed forces give rise to it. The light of this higher awareness also reveals an entirely new kind of understanding, instantly empowering us to act decisively to rebalance—and to restore harmony—to any of our relationships into which it is brought to bear.

Revealed: The Invisible Law Behind All Loving Relationships

Imagine that you and your partner have gone out for the evening with another couple, or perhaps with a small group of close friends. Maybe you're at an intimate bar, a dance place, or just out somewhere to dine.

The atmosphere and conversation are light; people are smiling, perhaps warmed by a glass of wine, or two. A few hours pass, the time grows late, and the waiter—maybe hoping to start clearing the table—comes over with the check. He's not sure who to hand it to, and so he stands there, feeling somewhat awkward.

For a moment, no one really wants to acknowledge that he's there. Most of the party looks in every direction but his, knowing that accidental eye contact might be interpreted by him as accepting responsibility for the bill. We've all been "there" in these moments…and unless our bank account is so flush that we don't care about the extra cost, and want to pay for the party, it's a slightly uncomfortable experience.

Maybe it's not every time, and maybe we're the kind of person who, wanting to disarm the discomfort, steps up to handle the situation; nevertheless, most of us have felt the tension that comes over the table when payment for the evening comes due.

Finally, someone at the table reaches over, saying, "Let me have it." At that point, he either announces, "This one is on me," receiving the chorus of "thanks" that follows; or he assumes the informal role of "party accountant," figuring out what each person must contribute to make good the amount owed.

This illustration seems simple enough on the surface; we've all been in that situation a hundred times. But just beneath this common experience—of an evening out with friends and being required to pay our fair share for that experience—is hidden a timeless law that exists for the sake of perfecting love. The extent of its influence reaches into and touches all of our relationships, but especially when it comes to the higher kind of love we want to share with our partner.

It's going to take some dedicated self-study to uncover and refine the riches of this celestial principle, but of this much, you may be assured: the more aware we become of this indwelling principle, including its ceaseless work to help balance and restore love in all of our relationships, the more empowered—freer—we will be to exchange patience for unkindness, understanding for blame, acceptance for rejection … even when our partner is unable to do the same.

Now, with this promise in mind, and to help us see the presence of this "celestial" principle hidden in the "common," let's return for a moment to our illustration of a night out with our friends.

Most would agree that when we go out to a restaurant for a nice meal, we never expect to dine or have drinks without having to pay for the services received. I understand, this seems so obvious as to not need to be stated. However, let's look a little deeper into this same exchange from another, higher point of view.

Whenever we take a seat in a restaurant or a bar, both of us—meaning the establishment, and ourselves—have already agreed to a certain unspoken relationship: they will provide us with food and service in exchange for a mutually agreed upon sum of money that we pay at evening's close.

This "balance due"—our "tab" not yet paid—represents a kind of momentary inequality between the establishment and us; it gave, we accepted. Services were rendered; paying our bill at the end of the evening balances our account; it reconciles any disparity between us, so that no one is indebted to the other in any way.

Now, if we take this illustration and superimpose its elements over our existing relationship with our partner, we'll see that there are many parallels between them.

For instance, just as there's that unspoken agreement between us and the restaurant—namely that they will do all that's in their power to see to our contentment—so do we have a similar kind of unspoken agreement with our partner. Only in this instance, not only do we expect "prompt service" and that our partner should always be "tableside," waiting to satisfy our needs—but, in our eyes, when they fail to do so, it breaks our agreement!

We all know, too well, that sense of being disappointed with the way our partner is performing—what it feels like to have our wishes or wants summarily dismissed, as if we amount to nothing in their eyes. And to the point of this parallel, in these moments we're struck with a strong sense of inequality between us, because our partner has failed to give us what we imagine is owed to us. And, just in case I need to repeat one of our earlier lessons, they feel exactly the same way about us. So both of us are thinking, if not speaking it aloud: "Look at all I do for you...and *this* is how you treat me?"

Isn't this a pretty fair description of what's going on behind the scenes of most of the fights we have with our partner? Sure, there are always extenuating circumstances: some old "stew" left unresolved, like a small event from the past that started as a molehill and grew into a mountain; or maybe an unintended act of inconsideration that stirs up memories of similar treatment, turning old embers into a flame. No matter how you slice these moments of suffering, one thing remains at their center, and it always comes down to this all-important point:

What difference does it make who starts a fight if both of us leave it feeling injured, still stinging from the blow of some perceived injustice delivered by our partner?

In truth, even if we "win" the argument, we never really escape the residue of negativity created by that encounter where, buried in the remnant of our momentarily resolved differences, a pain lives on that can only be blamed on the one felt to be responsible for it: our partner. So that even though the moment of contention has passed, a sense of imbalance lingers on. Each of us is still sure that the other remains in debt. They "owe" us something that can't quite be named but that experience has proven, time and time again, can never really be "paid off" as imagined.

Here's the point: the continuing pattern of "fight and make up" *isn't going to change by itself...* because the heartache and pain in our relationships is downstream from the unconscious parts of us that continue to create it. This means that no "payment"—no final apology we extract from our partner—has the power to "finally" resolve the differences we perceive as being between us. Here's why:

No matter how many times our partner agrees to appease us with an apology, regardless of the form it takes, *it is powerless to change the unconscious parts of us that resurface, or remain to find fault with them.*

This last insight deserves our attention. It means that our "go-to" conclusion about what divides us can no longer be pinned on just our partner. It means the unseen root in our conflict is a set of unconscious, ever-changing demands that our partner be and do as we want them to be... *in that moment!*

As just one example, haven't you ever noticed how one day, you might feel some twinge of resentment toward your partner for not giving you the attention or affection you're *sure* you need, and the next day be irritated with them for not giving you enough space! Small wonder we drive each other crazy!

Seeing the truth of this kind of pattern is the first step in being able to change it. We've reached the point now where we are ready to begin the practice of "relationship magic" because we realize that when it comes to being partners with the one we love...*each of us is responsible for whatever may be happening to both of us.*

In the short, true story that is coming up at the start of chapter 6, we will witness, firsthand, how this precious higher self-knowledge can empower us to turn any painful argument into an act of unconditional love.

Helpful Questions and Answers

Question: My partner and I have always had a pretty strong relationship. But, of late, and there's no explanation for it—at least not one that I can see—it takes fewer and fewer things that she does, or doesn't do, to bother me...more and more! I'm mature enough to know that I must have some hand in this growing sense of disappointment, but I just don't know where it is that I'm complicit. Can you help?

Answer: The following may take a little extra thought on your part, but I promise you that if you will consider the truth that it reveals—to you, about yourself—it will help release you from this growing resentment that you feel toward your partner. The only thing that troubles us about our partner...*is what* we *want from them.* In this one insight is also hidden the secret of how we can begin to drop the blame game, and to start taking full responsibility for ourselves.

Question: My boyfriend is so quick to go on the defensive that, I swear, all I have to do is even hint that there's something that I want to talk to him about and he lashes out at me...before I've even said a word. And sometimes he'll go on the attack in the middle of a simple conversation, when I haven't touched on anything like the topic he then accuses me of bringing up. I'm at a loss for how to understand this condition, let alone how to deal with it properly.

Answer: The following insight should help you see the real reason for his seemingly inexplicable behavior toward you. Being able to understand the unconscious forces behind this aggressive behavior is the same as developing the patience and compassion you'll need to stop resisting it, and that's the first step in breaking its pattern.

Most people "pounce" on others without provocation *not* because they want to cause pain, but because *they're afraid of being hurt*. Your boyfriend isn't actually trying to attack you, but rather he's temporarily under the negative influence of a fearful part of himself that feels it must defend itself from some forthcoming imagined pain. In the eyes of this unconscious level of self, the best way to protect itself is to be the first to attack. The more you learn to see his troubled action toward you as being the misplaced fear that it is, the easier it becomes not to resist it by returning some unkindness for the same. The less you resist, the greater his chance to see that you're not the enemy he's imagined you to be.

KEY LESSONS

1. Whoever would set blame upon another for feeling misunderstood, or who becomes bitter toward those thought to have let him down, has failed to realize the following self-liberating truth: the first root of sorrow in this life is not for what others have or have not done to us. Our suffering over the "shortcomings" of others is nothing less than the stuff of what we have yet to understand about ourselves.

2. Within us dwells an unconscious level of self that—for the most part—doesn't like *anything* that it sees. This helps explain why it spends as much time as it does remembering the things it doesn't like in our partner. If we want our relationship to grow beyond

the limitation inherent in the view of our unconscious nature, then our task is clear: we must choose to illuminate this negative nature, and part ways with it.

3. The less we try to "teach" others about *their* shortcomings, the more insights we'll gain into our own.

6

Your Relationship Can Only Be as New as You Are Willing to Be

There was a married couple with some real relationship issues. For the purposes of this teaching story, we'll call them Kathy and Stan. Perhaps you know a twosome just like them: sweet and loving to one another one moment, the next... well, you get the picture. They were always on the verge of a final crash onto the rocks, but steering away just in time to live and fight another day. They both knew just how slender was the thread of love keeping them together, which is why after most fights would come ample apologies, gifts or favors granted, and the usual attempt to start over. And that's where this story actually begins:

After a pretty rough week between them, Stan wants to make amends for all the tension he's been bringing home with him from the office, where things haven't been going well for him. Perhaps that's why he's been venting at the smallest provocation.

So he asks Kathy out for a dinner at their favorite place. In fact, it's the very spot where he had asked her to marry him some ten years past. His main thought is, if they could share a fine bottle of wine, talk quietly through some of the recent issues between them, there'd be a good chance of making things right again.

Later that evening, they return back to the house, and things could not have gone better. Both are feeling the warmth of a love they'd almost forgotten between them, and each is privately entertaining the idea that "just maybe" it would be possible to forgive and to forget all that had gone wrong up until now. He suggests they share a last glass of wine to commemorate the evening, and heads into the kitchen pantry to grab a bottle of their favorite wine from the cooler. She goes upstairs, into the bedroom, to freshen up a bit.

As he walks into the kitchen, his mind starts trying to recall an old pop song he used to like to sing along with many years back; something about "making a change, do things right." He feels the need to be different, not just for his own sake, but also for all those he loves. Everything seems in order; he even does a little dance step as he stands there, scanning the shelves for the right wine. His heart is happy. And then...his eyes fall on an open package of his favorite cookies.

In an instant, the box is in his hand, and in his other hand a cookie is on its way into his mouth. But he stops himself halfway there, laughing to himself at how easily he forgot why he was in the pantry in the first place. Almost at the same moment he remembers how many times his wife has asked him not to eat cookies before he goes to bed, not because she would deny him the pleasure, but because cookies late at night upset his stomach, causing him to toss and turn all night. And he decides on the spot, "I'm going to give up this habit once and for all. It will make her happy, not to mention help me lose a few pounds."

As he stands there, proud of his new found conviction, another thought comes to him: "Seen it too many times; no way to trust myself…better just throw these cookies away."

So he walks out of the pantry and over to the trash can under the kitchen sink. Opening the lid of the can, he's ready to throw in the cookies, including the one still in his hand. But then it whispers to him: *"No, don't waste me, eat me. One won't hurt anything. Besides your wife is still upstairs."* And on its heels, he thinks to himself, "Well, you know—one cookie. How bad could *that* be for me?"

Now, as he stands there—caught between a cookie and his wish to make a real change in his life for the sake of making his wife happy—here is what he doesn't know:

While on her way downstairs to meet him in the living room, his wife opened up her Facebook page where she sees that one of her best friends—someone she had trusted with a personal secret—just posted it for the world to see. In an instant, the tenderness that had been stirring in her heart is washed by a mixture of shame and anger; resentment begins to rage. With her mind still in an uproar, and hoping to find some relief in whatever advice she can get from her husband, she turns the corner into the kitchen from the living room. And what does she see?

There in the kitchen, with what looks like a cookie on its way into his mouth, is Stan. He sees her at the same time, and freezes like a deer caught in the headlights. He doesn't know what else to do except put a weak smile on his face. An awkward, strained silence fills the space between them. He cracks under the pressure, and begins to defend himself, stumbling over his own words, making everything worse:

"Kathy, this is not what it looks like. I mean it, I was doing this for you!"

Now, she looks at him like he's a madman, saying: "What? You're telling me that you're eating those cookies for me?"

"No, that's not what I meant to say. You don't understand. I was just about to throw all these cookies away when you came into the kitchen, I swear it!"

But all she can hear are his same old excuses.

And seeing her disdain for him, that disappointed look on her face that he's seen a hundred times, is too much for him. He wants to explain, but all that comes out of his mouth are defensive remarks, followed by whatever offense he can mount given his position of feeling wrongly attacked.

This storm pattern is prearranged. Unkind, demeaning remarks roll off their tongues without effort, each fueling a fire that wouldn't even exist were it not for the accidental coincidence of two unrelated events: she feeling hurt and betrayed by a friend, and he in the momentary grip of a second thought that caused him to pause just before he would throw the cookies away.

Cancel These Three Painful Patterns Before They Get Started

At this point—and now caught up in the heat of exchanging inflammatory remarks—neither one of them *actually* knows what they're fighting over ... or for. It's not inaccurate to say that an unconscious pain in Kathy is fighting with a similar characteristic in Stan. And as each tries, in vain, to overcome its counterpart, all that happens is that these opposing forces escalate their struggle.

Both feel wronged by their partner and are now demanding "payment" for the pain they feel unjustly inflicted upon them. History proves they will argue until this well-established pattern completes itself, one way or another. At some point, unable to resolve who's to blame for the pain, one or the other will either storm off to brood over the mistreatment, or decide that "retreat" is the better part of valor and make some kind of peace offering, perhaps an apology. Sad but true to say: in the long run, neither of these "solutions" makes any real difference. Their suffering passes into the night, but not the unseen reasons for it.

This situation sounds familiar, doesn't it? One event, a single word or critical glance, triggers a negative reaction. Then and there we feel our partner has set him- or herself against us, and—a moment later—we respond in kind. The feeling of being disrespected or misjudged morphs into a certainty that we've been betrayed; pain, not love, becomes our common denominator.

At this point, both parties are sure there's only one way out of this misery … and that's to get the offending party to acknowledge his or her misstep. The only way things can ever be right again is for them to make the appropriate confession *and* concession. But let's be quite clear about the following:

These unconscious demands, and the unhappy results they create, do nothing to actually balance the account we keep with those we feel are responsible for our pain. Our own past experience proves this is true: has any apology extracted from our partner ever changed the fact that—before too long—will come the inevitable demand for another one?

For our love to thrive, *everything* about this kind of pain-driven pattern must be shattered. Not one part of it can remain in place or else—like the root of an invasive weed left in the ground—the sorrow will surface some-where else under a different name, and continue to darken the hearts of those involved.

The stage is being set for the main lesson in this chapter. We now understand that acting from *any* part of this old pattern—while hoping for a new result—is like polishing old shoes that no longer fit, hoping the shine will change how they feel when you put them on! Following are three simple examples of such futile actions:

Painful Pattern #1

How many times have you either heard it said, or spoken these words yourself, near the "end" of a disagreement with your partner that has no end in sight: "Let's agree to disagree."

Now, *maybe* this technique has some benefit if you're at a party and, for the sake of illustration, let's say you're affiliated with a political group that's the opposite of the person you've found yourself talking to—face to face—"debating" the two disparate platforms. A few glasses of wine later, the intelligent discussion turns into a real disagreement. Finally comes the last resort, the socially accepted escape clause for conflicting opinions: "Let's just agree to disagree," and so you both go your separate ways, secretly hoping your paths never have to cross again.

But what happens when encounters like this come up with our partner where, because of something they've done, or refuse to do, there's a conflict between us—where we want them to agree that the problem at hand is *their* fault, but that's not how they see it? The fallback pattern of "agreeing to disagree" does nothing to change the one-sided parts within us whose false perceptions and demands set us against each other in the first place. How can we know this is true? Because each time we run into anything like the event that set this original disagreement into motion, it's not our "agreement" that we revisit; rather, it is we who are visited by the "wind and fury" of opposing forces whose continuing collision ensures that our original confrontation goes on ... and on.

Painful Pattern #2

Pretend that you don't feel any pain because of whatever just happened between you and your partner. Put on an unflustered face; show that what they've done "doesn't really matter."

Here's why this "act as if you don't care" routine seems to work, *at first*: parading an icy heart not only goes to show that you can't be hurt, but has the added "benefit" of making your partner feel the very chill you're giving off. Sounds strong, in theory; but, to paraphrase a timeless truth: *A stone hidden* beneath *the earth weighs as much as one on the surface.* In other words, just because we can pretend not to feel pain doesn't mean we're not suffering. Out of sight may seem out of mind, but the heart knows better, and grows bitter for whatever pain is buried in it.

Too soon, when this weight gets too great to bear—which it *always* does—everything that had been buried comes rushing to the surface. Pent-up resentment is released that's so far out of proportion to the deed blamed for it as to shake the very core of even the sturdiest of our relationships.

PAINFUL PATTERN #3

When all other approaches prove powerless, accuse your partner of having "changed." Find some way to imply, or even state directly, that what's gone wrong in the relationship is basically their fault: "something" has happened to them, and that they no longer care for you, as was once true. In other words, try to make your partner feel guilty because they've been unable to satisfy the expectations you have placed on them.

This pattern of using guilt or shame to "reshape" our partner is doomed at the outset. Even if we manage to momentarily make them into the "perfect partner," the ensuing contentment of having our expectations met is unsustainable; *not* just because our partner is unable to maintain the makeover we've imagined will end our differences, but because there's no satisfying the parts of ourself that almost always *find something that needs to be "fixed" in those we love.* This pattern of using guilt or shame to try to change our partner will never come to an end until we see that it's not just our partner who's weaving it!

A short summary of these last few insights brings us to a fairly stunning discovery: our partner is not—as we're presently inclined to believe—the reason why any painful pattern keeps reappearing in our relationship.

To be sure, those we love are as much at "fault" for whatever makes us "crazy," as we are driven "mad" by their actions. But the real reason behind the nature of any escalating conflict between us is… *we don't know what to do with* our own *pain*. Trying to escape its pressure is what pushes us to try to "remake" our partner or—at the very least—to make them "pay" for the suffering that we're sure they're making us feel.

Two Steps to a New Relationship With Your Partner *and* Yourself

In the largely autobiographical film *Peaceful Warrior*, loosely based on the book *Way of the Peaceful Warrior* by author Dan Millman, we meet a mysterious old man, a delightful character by the name of Socrates who operates a run-down gas station. The story line revolves around the relationship that Socrates develops with Dan. As the plot develops, and Dan learns to trust the old man, Socrates takes him through a series of powerful experiences and challenging life lessons all designed to achieve a single end: to help Dan realize and then release himself from a set of largely self-imposed limitations carried over from his past. At an inflection point in one of their dialogues—

to help strengthen the point he wanted to make of a particular lesson—Socrates tells Dan:

"The secret to change is to focus all of your energy, not on fighting the old, but on building the new." [5]

This idea seems simple enough to understand and, at one level, it is. But hidden within it is also a secret instruction that, once revealed, will help us see the way out of any and all old patterns we may be reliving with our partner. Study the following insight closely; read and reread it as needed until some of its higher understanding reaches the part of yourself able to employ its power.

At the outset of feeling any disagreement about to begin—whether we're about to go on the offensive, or find ourselves on our heels, feeling defensive—we must have enough awareness of ourselves to realize this very simple truth: in that same moment *there is only one of two things* that can be causing this conflict. Either an unseen part of us has acted to start this conflict, or some unconscious part of us has been stirred into opposing a similar characteristic in our partner. As long as we remain unaware of this "starting gun" that sets us racing to win the argument, we'll continue to see everything about the moment from one side only: our side. But here's the truth, as well as the explanation for why no one can ever win such a race:

---

5. Dan Millman, *Way of the Peaceful Warrior* (Novato, CA: HJ Kramer, 1980).

Both of these actions—whether an unseen part of us steps up to initiate the pattern, or steps back to resist an equally unwitting action instigated by our partner—*are a part of the overall pattern.* In other words, the real reason this negative pattern keeps being resurrected is that, over and over again, we identify with one side or the other of these opposing forces. Take away *either one* of these two sides and well, you've heard the old expression: "what if they gave a war, and no one came?" This is why as soon as we catch the smallest hint of impatience, a mounting frustration, or any sense of resentment gathering steam we must act—decisively—as outlined here in the following two steps.

STEP #1

The moment we can be aware of any negative thought or feeling looking to dig up a familiar reason to blame our partner for something, we must work to instantly drop these troublemakers, much as we would a hot skillet that we know will burn our hand if we hold on to it.

After all, now that we're aware of how these opposing forces draw us into *their* struggles—trying to set us against each other—we know better than to take *their* part in any pattern they seek to create within us. And yet, as liberating as this first step may be, it's only a hint, the herald of a still greater power to come.

STEP #2

Now that we're becoming aware of these opposing forces, and how they trick us into identifying with *their* struggles—setting us at odds with our partner—the stage is set to turn our higher self-understanding into this completely new action.

The more we study the wisdom of this next insight, agreeing to embrace the truth it reveals, the more we will find ourselves with the power we need to shatter any punishing pattern before it begins:

The instant we become aware of any opposing force at work in us—some negative thought or feeling wanting us to embrace its agitation—not only must we drop it on the spot, but *we must also drop any familiar sense of self that has appeared with it in that same moment.* Here's a short illustration that shows why we must detect and then reject this false identity.

Imagine you're walking down the street, maybe after dinner, and you're window-shopping with your partner. Things couldn't be nicer, and you're feeling a quiet sense of gratitude for all that life and love have given to you. Then he says, out of the blue, something like: "You know, I've been thinking about it, and we really need to cut down on our expenses." *Say what?*

In less than a heartbeat, gone is that contented sense of yourself—the "you" that just a moment before didn't have a care in the world. Its been replaced by a smoldering sense of discontent with your partner as well as "the whole situation"! You've gone from being mild Dr. Banner to the angry "Hulk," and the only one who sees this terrible transformation is your partner, who suddenly wishes he were anywhere else but standing next to you! Here's the point of this illustration:

Not only weren't you feeling anything like a "Hulk" before his ill-conceived words were spoken, *but neither did there exist that agitated sense of yourself* that's now advocate for, and defender of, some aggressive negative state!

This false sense of self is now in charge. In such moments—being now unconsciously identified with a host of negative thoughts and feelings—whatever they oppose, you do too; their nature has become as your own. They call the shots: cruel things are said; actions soon regretted are taken. And yet, the only power this painful pattern has to keep you in its grip comes from but one place: your identification with the negative forces that are keeping it in play. So, rather than identifying with these unconscious parts of yourself that want to justify being negative…say goodbye to them instead. Choose to snap the spell of this false sense of self by deliberately dropping any dark inner dialogue it may be trying to drag you into as to "why" you have to set things straight. Be vigilant with this new kind of inner resolve and you'll soon see your negative state—and the false sense of self that embraces it—fade away. Their disappearance is the same as dropping the painful pattern that *they* were trying to keep alive.

Why Old "Tried and True" Solutions Leave You "Black and Blue"

Now that we've just about reached the end of this chapter, it's time to put all of the insights and principles we've just studied into personal practice. We're ready for our first look at a real-time application of relationship magic.

To that end, let's pick up where we left off in our earlier story when Kathy caught her husband, Stan, with his hand in the proverbial "cookie jar."

Just as a brief refresher: we left them standing there, face-to-face, on the verge of a fight that was the last thing either of them had expected that evening. Already in pain from feeling betrayed by her friend, Kathy catches Stan in what seems to be an act of breaking his promise to her. Caught off guard, Stan can't believe that she could be so quick to misjudge him.

While the particular conditions that bring a moment like this to pass might belong to almost any set of coincidences, the outcome remains the same. The pattern of their conflict is prearranged, virtually guaranteed, by all of their earlier disagreements that went unresolved; not unlike a steam kettle—on a slow but steady heat—that finally reaches its inevitable boiling point. Only now, in this instance—and all due to the unfortunate coincidence of two unrelated events—they stand there, glaring at one another, each waiting for their partner to admit the whole painful mess is their fault! And the whole time, both are thinking:

"You owe me an apology for this pain in me; it's *your* responsibility—as my partner—to make things right between us."

We all should know—from having been in similar situations—what comes next if the above demand goes unanswered. The fight escalates until the first part of the pattern plays itself out when—unable to deal with the stress between them—one of them storms away. But the unresolved pain—the opposing forces ultimately responsible for each of these provisional splits between them—lives on to fight another day. Like a kind of dark seed, it waits for the conditions it needs to reappear and play out its uncontested part in a pattern that never seems to come to an end.

It's with a measure of trust that I ask the following question: can we see something of our own relationships by looking at them through the eyes of Kathy and Stan? If so, two things should be fairly obvious:

First, any ongoing dispute we may have with our partner can't come to an end until one of us sees that our usual "tried and true" solutions to unsettled differences do nothing to *really* resolve them. On the contrary, our standard "fix" is actually an unseen part of the very pattern in which we're stuck! And that brings us to the second obvious point that I promised to reveal above:

The clearer our insight into the real nature of this trap—including our unseen role in it—the nearer we are to enacting the following understanding that alone can shatter it. The only way some painful pattern with our partner, or with anyone for that matter, can come to a true stop is *if one of us agrees to shoulder the burden of shattering it completely.*

This new action has nothing to do with another level of apology; nor is it based in some promise to be a better person. It is an act of love that has *nothing* to do with the past or the future. It is timeless, true, and unfailing in its power to put things right between you and your partner, even if your partner fails to recognize it as being so the moment you enact it.

To see what this kind of love "looks like," and to witness its power to shatter a punishing pattern in our relationship before it begins, let's look at this alternative ending to the story of Kathy and Stan.

Stan's back is arched in defiance of Kathy's reproach at finding him "cookie in hand," and she's midway in turning her back on him, about to walk away from a pain she can't deal with again. In that same moment, something unthinkable happens to Stan. There's no saying how such miracles come to happen, only that they do when the time is right for the one involved.

Rising up and out of his own heated thoughts and feelings—almost like a cool breeze that's out of place moving across a hot desert floor—a flight of unfamiliar thoughts catches Stan's attention. It calms his agitated mind, stopping him from firing back words that would have only made things worse between them. There are really no words for such an impression, but if we had to squeeze the whole of it into that moment it announced itself, here's what it had to say:

"This just *can't* be right; how can our perfect evening be reduced to rubble over nothing real? What is this thing that keeps coming between us to wreck our love?"

And on the heels of these same thoughts came another impression, a feeling unlike any he'd ever known before. It was one part declaration, the other an assertion with a strength that startled him—it was loud and clear:

"This has gone too far, and I won't be a part of it anymore. If things between us don't change right now, right here, they never will."

The next moment, and almost before he even knows he is speaking, he says: "Kathy, wait... please; don't walk away. I have something that I have to tell you.

Of course, she's heard words just like these countless times before. What they usually mean is that you haven't heard all I have to say on this subject, and neither of us is going to have any peace until I've finished what I have to say!

But this time, something *is* different. There's a different tone, a kind of tenderness in his voice she's never heard before, and it stops her. She turns around to face him, the space between them already less than what it was the moment before.

Stop Any Argument By Using These Five Simple Words

At first, fearing to see a "certain look" on his face that she's grown to know she doesn't want to see, Kathy is unable to look Stan directly in the eye. He knows it, too, and begins walking toward her, saying:

"Kathy, please, don't look away; not this time."

She yields to his request, and when she raises her eyes to look at him, she's surprised to see his eyes have no trace of the anger in them that was there only moments before.

He walks over to her and stretches out his hands for hers, and she takes an involuntary step back.

"I want to tell you something that's really important." He holds out his hands again.

With that, she puts her hands into his hands, and searches his eyes with her own. There's nothing in them that wants to punish her. In a single breath, her body relaxes. And now her eyes begin to question his. Without words they're asking him:

"What's going on here?" And he answers her, as if he can hear exactly what she's thinking. A partial smile crosses his face, and he says:

"I get it now."

"Get what?"

"The whole reason this pattern keeps repeating itself: fighting over what usually amounts to nothing, making up, getting mad again, both of us caught up in that terrible feeling as if our life depends on hearing the other admit they're wrong. Do you know what I mean?"

"…For the most part, but I'm not exactly sure what you're trying to tell me."

"Look Kath, I can't speak for you, but I have to assume you feel the same way I do since we keep finding ourselves in these stand-offs. In my mind, and now I can see that it runs through the background of every argument we've ever had, there's this feeling that *you owe me*; it's as if there's something in me that can't rest until you've made right all the wrongs I think you've ever done to me. I'm not saying this is a right feeling…just that I see it's always been there."

He pauses for a moment, looks at her, and sees that she's wearing that quirky smile of hers that he's always loved; it gives him the go-ahead to continue:

"…So, if you feel like I do, and how could it be otherwise, then we've got nowhere to go other than the same place we've just come to again: another fight, another stalemate. And that's why it's become so clear to me now:

"This whole painful pattern can never come to an end *as long as I cling to any demand that you make good on a debt…a debt that can't exist outside of some imagined payment overdue.* And neither can I ever pay off that kind of debt to you; it's impossible."

"I'm not sure…I mean, if what you've said is true, then…where does that leave us?"

"Don't you see? The *whole* of this kind of imagined debt between us has to be paid off *now*, not later; otherwise, this pain—including the pattern that keeps it alive—is *never* going to end. I don't know why I never could see this before, but it doesn't matter because now I do. I know what I have to do to make things right between us."

"What are you talking about, Stan?"

"I'm not that sure how to explain it in words, but the best I can tell you is that *I'm* going to make the payment it takes to make things right between us, *right now.*

She looks at him, not at all sure what he's telling her. "What are you talking about, what does that mean, 'you're going to make the payment due'?"

"I'm not going to fight with you. Not now, not over this, in fact, not over anything ever again. I know, I know…you can be as mad at me as you want to be, and odds are I may deserve it; but regardless of what you choose to do, I'm going to make good this debt between us, because it has to be paid off. So, I'm picking up the tab for this evening's troubles; *this one is on me.*

Before Kathy even knows she's going to say something, a short string of angry word comes flying out of her mouth:

"I don't think so, mister; if that's supposed to be some kind of apology, it's not that simple; I caught you breaking a promise you made to me."

"I know it looked that way to you, but even so... whether you mistook my action, or even if I did slip up, none of that matters anymore."

"If *that* doesn't matter, then what does?"

"Love, Kathy; *that's* what matters; the love that brought us together, and that I believe has the power to keep us together... but only if we make the sacrifices we need to keep it alive. That's why... *this one is on me.*"

Experience the Living Heart of Relationship Magic

It's my hope that you—the reader—were able to make this important journey of self-discovery illustrated in this relationship between Kathy and Stan. For one thing, it should be clear how these unseen opposing forces not only stir up the conflicts that they do, but also that as long as we remain unaware of some unwanted pattern they help renew, they will keep working behind the scenes to ensure its painful continuity.

Yet, as vital as these last few summary insights may be, even more important to us is to get to the heart of Stan's great realization that took place at the end of the story.

The following two short paragraphs reveal the hidden meaning of what Stan hoped to convey to Kathy when he told her: "I'm going to make the payment that's overdue; this one is on me."

I accept full responsibility for anything that I may have ever done to hurt you; I see now that these unconscious parts of myself didn't know any better than to blame you for their pain. But, thankfully, I have just realized that who I am, my true Self, is more than any one of these conflicted parts. And now I willingly agree to pay, not only for what these unconscious parts of myself have done in the past to cause you pain, but for any time to come... should I forget what I have now seen is true.

So, you see, I'm not giving myself up to you, or even for you; it's much more than that. I'm giving up the parts of myself that I now see cannot take our relationship any deeper, any further into love. And I agree to make this payment for a love that has made it possible for me to see that if I don't... our love won't survive.

In every great story throughout time—whether we examine the path of Siddhārtha, destined to become the Buddha; the trials of Moses; the sacrifices of Jesus Christ, Mohammed, Saint Teresa of Ávila, Gandhi; the lives of Oskar Schindler, Martin Luther King—all the way to and through the mythical character of Aslan in C. S. Lewis's *The Chronicles of Narnia*—all of the heroic characters share one thing in common: each goes through a distinctly memorable moment of transformation where, in one way or another, they say and then act upon these words: "*This one is on me.*"

These timeless stories resonate with us the way they do because—at least in part—*they are the same as our story.*

We are each and all, at once, not just the instrument of opposing forces, and the reluctant witness of what, left unchecked, they always do; but within us also lives a higher order of love that alone has the power to reconcile these same unconscious states and "make right whatever wrong" they may have wrought. So, let me assure you of one last thing before we close out this chapter:

I know how impossible it feels in the middle of a knock-down, drag-out fight with your partner to be aware of *any* kind of love. Nevertheless, be encouraged: the more you'll contemplate the possibility of, and then work at, this practice of "making the payment due," the more you'll come to see the fact of the following truth that helps set you free.

Love is always present whenever, and wherever, opposing forces meet. It is never farther away than your willingness to remember it in the midst of whatever that trial by fire may be. This means that everything depends on what *you choose to put first* in these moments, because in the end, when it comes to painful relationship patterns, there really are only two choices:

We can either take the path of least resistance, and become the unwitting instrument of a familiar pain that *will* reincarnate both itself and the pattern within which it breeds its discontent, or we wake up and follow this new path all the way to its higher possibilities.

As soon as we start to feel some old familiar stress or strain when we're around our partner, we realize it's time to "go to work." Now, instead of mechanically identifying with that familiar old pain that's "asking" us to see our partner as the one responsible for our pain, we see the lower nature within us, inviting us down a one-way street that dead-ends in another fight. And seeing the truth of this unconscious part of us, we give it up. *That's the payment.* It's a kind of sacrifice that only love can make; and our agreement to enact this new understanding guarantees the growth of our partnership through a continual rebirth of it.

Helpful Questions and Answers

Question: My partner and I seem to be stuck in a rut. We both realize the need to start over, to let go and let love guide us through the rocky moments we keep coming to. But here's the deal: when push comes to shove—one of us always brings up something the other did in days past to "prove" that they were wrong then, so now they have to be wrong again! This is a painful pattern that both of us see as a major stumbling block to our love, but we're clueless how to break it.

Answer: Here's a helpful hint provided for us by English author T. H. White, famous for his series of novels about King Arthur, which were collected together in *The Once and Future King*. He writes: *"Let us now start fresh without remembrance, rather than live forward and backward at the same time. We cannot build the future by avenging the past."*

Wishing to bring an end to some painful pattern with our partner by identifying with the unconscious "remembrance" of all of the reasons they are at fault is like hoping to escape the wrath of a storm by walking out into it. Before any unwanted pattern can come to an end, one of the parties in it has to see, and then give up, the parts of themself helping to weave it … again.

Question: I fear that if I don't stand up for my rights, especially in the midst of a fight, my husband will see this as a sign of weakness and literally start thinking he can just walk all over me anytime he so chooses. And yet, honestly, after an argument—even when I get my way—I still feel like I've been trampled by a stampede of wild beasts! What am I missing?

Answer: There's an Aesop's fable about a bull and a lion getting ready to fight with one another over who will drink from a small pool of water they both want to possess. Above them, in a tree, sits a smiling vulture, excited to watch them go into mortal combat. It knows that whichever one wins, "dinner" will soon be served!

The meaning of this story is, stay out of any war between opposing forces, as all you can do is become a casualty of *their* unconscious combat. Call upon your higher awareness of the unconscious "lion and bull" within you to help you stay out of *their* struggle. As you learn to observe these negative states, sacrificing the parts of yourself that tend to unconsciously identify with them, not only will you rise above their conflict, but your struggle to do so will also give your husband the opportunity *he* needs to see, and then to let go of, his part in any such confrontation. However, should your husband prove incapable of seeing the good of your efforts to instrument your new understanding—so that he continues to try and force his will on you—that's another story; one that only you can read as it unfolds. So, let's be clear: it's your life, not his to use as he pleases. Do all you can to walk through your differences together; but, if need be, walk away from anyone who abuses you…in any way.

KEY LESSONS

1. No one is willing to risk losing a "fight" until he or she sees that there's nothing to be gained by going another ten rounds in the same ring.

2. Behind every expectation we have for how we should be treated by others lurks the inevitable sense

of feeling betrayed by them any time they fail to hit their assigned mark. Behind this disappointment in their character—in fact, its partner in this kind of bias—dwells an unseen sense of righteousness based on a false assumption that we are nothing like what we are so easily moved to judge.

3. There are times when the greatest strength or kindness we can possess is to allow our partner their weakness without pointing it out, or otherwise trying to punish them for it. Acts of love such as these cost us a part of ourselves, and when we agree to pay this price it is a better, brighter relationship that we buy back.

7

Take the Upper Path That Leads to Perfect Love

We've been looking at the various ways that opposing forces act to determine how we experience our partner, as well as how the unseen interaction of these forces can literally change—moment to moment—the very nature of our relationship. Here are a few simple examples of how their interplay produces the results they do, as in when "opposites attract."

For instance, when a loved one embraces us with a smile, we feel *drawn to them*; but when our partner snaps at us, and "opposites collide," we're filled with an immediate *resistance...ready for a fight.*

Thankfully, as we've been learning, there is also a third and reconciling force, one that exists to "balance" these opposing forces, to make good whatever may be the momentary difference between them.

We know this third force mostly by the feeling we have of its presence in our heart. This celestial characteristic expresses itself through our wish to find an enduring way to *resolve* any painful sense of difference between our partner and us; to close the distance we feel from one another that's been created by taking one side or the other of the opposing forces.

We can also call this power unconditional love. It is, by nature, impersonal in that its only "interest" in any interaction with opposing forces is to unite and harmonize them by seeing to their integration.

In nature, the interplay of these three forces creates all the familiar patterns that we see everywhere around us: waves of any kind; spirals that we often see in seashells; meanderings, as in flowing rivers and streams; symmetry, in the left and right sides of our body or the branching of trees; and other forms too numerous to mention. But these celestial forces, and the forms they create, *are powerless to change their own patterns*; they can only repeat themselves. We can illustrate this truth by looking at what's likely a familiar experience with our partner.

Let's say we're out somewhere together for a light evening meal, or maybe just taking an early morning walk. From out of the blue, our partner makes a dark remark of some kind. A part of us reacts; it instantly opposes their negative state. A moment later, without any further thought on our part, we reach the mistaken conclusion their offhand comment means they'd rather be anywhere else in the world but with us.

Now, as a result of our mistaken perception, a pained reaction rifles through us that we fire off at them in the form of a dark glance. They see the way we look at them, and the force of our unmasked negativity hits its mark. Instantly, they resist this feeling, and react by trying to escape its distress. But the only way they know to get rid of it is to blame us for it. The greater grows the pitch of this pain and blame, the less chance there is of understanding— and resolving—our differences *because this kind of pain* is unaware of—unable to *see*—anything *other than what it wants*.

With the above in mind, the following insight should be clear: to have any hope of reconciling, harmonizing this situation—where the pain born of it *not only blinds us, but also binds us* to the unconscious forces responsible for every such useless fight—we're going to need a new set of "eyes" through which to look at it!

Don't let this unusual idea of a "new set of eyes" throw you. It's a beautiful, timeless notion that runs, like a golden thread, through all true religious and spiritual teachings, east and west. But, for now, let's just take these words "new eyes" to mean the same as being able to look at our relationship through a set of *new ideas*, unlike any we may have come across before.

These new ideas belong to a higher part of our own heart and mind that isn't limited in the same way as is our lower nature that can only see one side—*its side*—of any unwanted moment with our partner. Rather, this higher level of self is able to look at *both sides* of any situation at the same time.

For example, we all know what happens when we realize that we've completely misjudged a friend, family member, or our partner. In that same moment of seeing our mistake, not only are we released from a false and painful sense of self—born of our "one-sided" view of the situation—but so also is everyone else who had been caught up in our misunderstanding.

Perhaps one of the most surprising things about revelations like these—as we stand in the light of our new understanding that "sets us free"—is how long it took for us to realize what was right before our eyes all along!

Now let's look at this last idea by deliberately recalling a kind of common experience, one whose pain should be familiar to us all: a quarrel of some kind with our partner. Only this time, let's look at it through the "eyes" of our new understanding that allows us to see something that we've likely never seen before.

Whenever we find ourselves in a fight of some kind, pretty much all we can see is who's to blame for the pain we feel. This pain-induced blindness does more than just pit us against one another. It also stands between us, blocking any awareness of a simple truth that—once realized—acts to change something deep within us: in any disputed moment with a loved one, we're not the only one suffering through it; *our partner is in pain ... too.*

A Simple Truth to Soften Even the Hardest of Hearts

An idea like the one above—that our partner suffers our disagreements as much as we do—may seem obvious to us when we're able to sit and calmly read about it. But, in the midst of some heated exchange, we have very little if any awareness of such matters.

I remember the first time I discussed an idea like the one above; a student had come to see me, asking for insight into an escalating argument between her and her partner. From what she explained, it seemed they couldn't get past the "same old argument" whose continuation she blamed squarely on him.

I can still see the look on her face when I suggested that "it takes two to tango," and that whatever pain she was in—as a result of their ongoing conflict—she could be sure that he was suffering it as well. That was when she looked me straight in the eye and asked, as if there was no other possible answer to her question:

"Why should I care about what *he's* going through when he's the one who keeps dragging us into the same stupid fight?"

Taking a deep breath, which I hoped would encourage her to do the same, I paused for a moment. It was clear that we wouldn't make any progress until the anger she was feeling was allowed to pass. After a few more seconds, I asked her a question of my own:

"Could this be pain doing the talking for you right now … saying you don't care that your partner is suffering as you are? Because I can be of no help to you, whatsoever, if what you're asking me to do is take your side in this matter. On the other hand, but only should you wish it, we can look at the *real* reason for what's going on between the two of you. Which is it to be?"

I could tell by her reaction that the message got through, and when her face relaxed for the first time since we sat down together, it seemed a clear sign that she was ready to listen, and to learn whatever she could.

"First, if we wish to love our partner unconditionally, meaning no matter what they manifest toward us—even if it seems uncaring—we must never return unkindness with unkindness. Can you see that nothing positive, helpful, let alone healing can ever come out of a negative reaction, regardless of how justified it may feel at the moment?

She nodded in silent agreement, and so I continued with my train of thought:

"That's why, even if we're yet unable to enact this kind of higher love, there must be no doubt in our mind as to the truth of the following idea:

"When we really love someone, whether it's our partner, a family member, or a close friend, *the last thing we want to do is to hurt them, to add any more pain to their life than they already have to bear.*"

I looked her in the eye: "Can you agree with me on this last point?"

It was clear that she was struggling with what I had just asked her to see: namely that love and resentment, kindness and cruelty, can never occupy the same space at the same time.

She looked at me, and then looked away. I could see that her mind was working overtime to resolve this contradiction I had pointed out to her in her behavior toward her partner.

Then she looked back at me, and I could tell by her stiffening expression that something in her decided it didn't like the direction our conversation was taking. A moment later, she asked the following question. See if it sounds familiar to you, too:

"I know that what you're saying is right, but how else do you expect me to feel when *he* is so wrong? There's one thing I know for sure: I'm not the one who picks the fight, who starts the pain train rolling down the track! So, if he's in the same kind of pain that I am—as you say he is—then I sure don't see it."

"Yes, that's the point; you can't see his pain *because he's already in it...*"

"What on earth do you mean by *that*?"

"Let's forget about him for a moment; we can best see what we need to by looking at ourselves in any moment when a disagreement first gets started. Haven't you ever wondered how your level of impatience, frustration, or just plain anger can go from zero to sixty miles an hour in less than a split second? How do you explain that?"

"I never really thought about it…"

"Exactly. All such negative states are 'powered' by one kind or another of an unseen, and therefore unresolved, pain that lives within us. Experience proves this true: just because the storm of some conflict has passed, even by mutual consent to 'just drop it,' it doesn't mean the cause of that argument has gone away. At the end of any confrontation between two people there's always a residue, some kind of grudge that goes 'underground,' just waiting for the right circumstances to come charging back out… to fight another day!"

"I'm not sure I understand."

"Any unresolved difference between you and your partner is like a grain of sand that slips inside an oyster's shell, settling into the folds of its flesh. Once lodged there, that tiny bit of sand becomes an irritant to the oyster whose only defense is to cover it with constant secretion. That's how pearls are formed, by the way!"

She looked at me and rolled her eyes, as if to say … "really?" But I knew she was getting the general idea, so I continued.

"Well, it's a rough analogy, but the point here is that unresolved issues between us and the one we love are … irritants. We even get used to living with them; that is, until some unwanted event brings them, and their pain, back to life. And when both partners carry the seeds of this kind of pain—born of whatever unsettled objections they still have with one another—then, as you've already seen, the smallest spark between the two of you can turn into a towering inferno."

Then I looked directly at her, and said: "It's true, isn't it?"

"Yes," she replied, somewhat reluctantly. "Who knew there is so much going on behind the scenes … let alone that it's happening in both of us?"

"Yes, good; you've just glimpsed the main point I hoped you might see: even before a fight, let alone afterward, *you and your partner are already living with a kind of pain that burdens both of you equally, and yet neither one of you knows that this is true about the other.* Which brings us full circle, and to an answer for your original question: why do my partner and I keep doing to each other what both of us say we don't want to do?"

Turn Heated Exchanges
Into Healing Turning Points

We can now start to see what would have been unimaginable to even consider before: regardless of our certainty as to which of us starts or rekindles a quarrel, *the real cause of the continuing conflict between us lies elsewhere.* Which is why, as strange as the following insight may seem at first, the importance of working to see the truth of it simply can't be overstated:

Despite any appearance to the contrary, it's not our partner, nor is it we who strikes the first blow in any dispute: *it's pain that picks the fight.*

No doubt this last idea challenges most of our familiar notions, especially when we're sure we've been wronged and feel that it's our right to seek whatever "justice" we might. But, putting all this aside for a moment, as we quietly study the secret cause of our struggles rather than being caught up in them, we should also be able to see and agree to the following:

Just as it's clear that we'd never hurt the one we love were it not for some pain pushing us to do so, *the same holds true for our partner.* So much depends on our being able to remember what our heart already knows is true: if love is that timeless divine force that unites and heals all that lives and breathes, then how can it ever be that which divides us? It can't; it's never love that fights. *Never.* With this last thought in mind, let's summarize the three new ideas that bring us to this critical juncture in our studies.

New Understanding #1

Let's say we have a "bone to pick" with our partner. This should be easy enough to imagine! Is this because we feel good about them in that moment? Or is it more likely that there's a pressure and a pain in us that "knows" who's to blame for it, and what they must do to make things right? The answer to this question is pretty obvious, which leads us directly to the insight that follows.

New Understanding #2

This particular pain that we feel in these moments doesn't exist without our partner being there—before us—either in body or in our mind. The same holds true for whatever pain our partner may experience in our presence; it doesn't exist without us being there in the same way. This means that even though there are two of us "there," between us *there is only one pain*. How can this be so? As the next point makes clear, it's all under celestial law.

New Understanding #3

Whatever we oppose in our partner causes our partner to oppose us; for instance, any time we oppose something about our partner's attitude, we can be sure our partner will oppose anything we have to say about that! *Pain opposes pain.* Which means that now we can see what we were unable to before: as long as we look at our partner as the one responsible *for the pain we're in*, we remain effectively blind to the one thing about this condition that we must see...if we're going to stop hurting one another:

Half the responsibility for this unwanted pattern—including the pain that helps keep it alive—belongs to us, and the other half belongs to our partner. In other words, the pain that first sets us against one another, only to push us apart, isn't his, or hers, or theirs. It's our pain.

There aren't words enough to explain how important it is that we *feel* the truth of the above summary insight. Only then will we be able to ask ourselves a question that unconscious pain is incapable of considering, let alone interested in answering. In truth, this is a question of conscience that maybe fewer than one in a hundred million of us have ever thought to ask ourselves. But, for those who wish to know a healthier, more loving relationship with our partner, we must dare to ask it of ourselves, and even better...right in the middle of a fight with our partner: *"Why is my pain more important than yours?"*

If we're both suffering for having been set against one another by unconsciously identifying with opposing forces, then we have to ask, especially if we love our partner as we profess to do: why do we feel as if our pain is more important than theirs?

When we really love someone, the last thing we want for him or her is to suffer. Who among us hasn't thought, upon seeing a loved one in the throes of some kind of pain, that if it only were in our power, we would gladly take their pain away by agreeing to make it our own?

And yet, though most of us have felt something of this higher wish—to surrender ourselves for the sake of love, regardless the personal cost—we've also witnessed our inability to do so; the truth is, when comes some trial by fire, little to nothing in us can remember what was foremost in our heart only moments before. And there's a good reason for this kind of spiritual amnesia:

This kind of unconscious pain that lives within us needs someone, something, to blame for it. And, in much the same way, blame must have pain in order to keep itself alive. These opposing sides are literally nothing without each other to maintain the misery that they create together. The more aware we can be of this unconscious partnership, the less tempted we are to want any part of it!

Study closely the following pair of summary insights for this chapter section. Learn to look at them as a single lesson and you will see how it's possible to turn any troublesome moment with your partner into a healing turning point for both of you.

SUMMARY INSIGHT #1

Any pain in us—that demands our partner pay for it—*can't heal itself*; if it could have, it would have long ago. Add to this fact—as we've seen is true—that whatever "payment" we'd exact from our partner in these moments not only does nothing to heal *their* pain but also, in fact, only aggravates it further! Which in turn...then turns on us, reseeding both of our suffering, and guaranteeing that same unwanted pattern is reborn.

SUMMARY INSIGHT #2

The unconscious pain that pushes us into, and then through the repetition of any unwanted pattern with our partner is, in fact, not what it seems. It is *not* proof of some irreconcilable difference between us, but rather *stands as evidence of something that lives in each of us, that we have in common.*

Even the faintest first stirring of this higher awareness—that whatever pain divides us is, in fact, a single pain shared between us—makes it possible for us to open our heart and mind to embrace a new idea that can't be reached in any other way.

We have but one, true hope of being able to rise above this unseen world of opposing forces that cannot heal themselves, let alone bring an end to the patterns they create each time they attempt to do so. It is time for us to learn how to call upon a "third" force: an altogether higher order of wisdom, compassion, and kindness whose singular power is not only to unify these opposing forces but, in the moment of their appearance, to complete the very purpose of their existence.

In truth, you already know this celestial force; its most common name is *love*. But let me ask you to suspend, at least for the rest of this chapter, *all* that you think you understand about it; for the "love" that we know, in whose name we call out what we now care for most, is to this higher order love that we're about to discover as a candle's light is to the light of the sun.

We're not talking about the kind of love we have for a delicious meal, a beautiful day, a family member, or even for our partner in the most tender of moments. We've already seen that this level of love can flip-flop into its opposite at the drop of a hat.

We're about to discover a level of love that can neither be imagined nor created. It can't be *made* to change a single unwanted moment into one that we want, even though that's the reason for its existence. And while we can't cause this higher order of love to appear at will, we can learn to understand, and eventually have full trust in, the following:

Whenever, and wherever, two or more of us are connected by a shared pain of some kind—as in a fight with our partner, or suffering some misfortune with loved ones or strangers alike, there is—already with us in that same moment—a higher love waiting to heal it, and to help make us whole at the same time.

The best way to illustrate the deep "relationship magic" in this last idea is to share a very personal story with you.

An Introduction to the Greatest Love of All

I can remember it as if it was yesterday, although more time than I can account for has passed since that telling moment. My voice had been persistently hoarse, a feature I'd made peace with due to my rigorous teaching schedule. However, given that it seemed a little worse than usual, I made an appointment to see an ear, nose, and throat specialist.

The doctor's office had the same smell as every doctor's office I'd ever visited, and walking into it made me want to walk out of it at first whiff. But, at this point, I knew that wasn't an option. So, after waiting the usual thirty to forty minutes, I was led to another, smaller room, where I waited again for the doctor who, as it turned out, was very kind.

After he used some special equipment to capture detailed images of my vocal cords, my wife and I waited for him to review the results. It was one of those moments when you know—just by looking at him—that he would rather not have to tell you what comes next. Sure enough: I was diagnosed with an early stage of cancer. Shock gave way to devastation.

It's hard to use the word "fortunate" to describe what took place over the next six months of my life, but I know that I was lucky to find myself in the hands of a very gifted physician, Dr. Clark Rosen, a specialist in his field. He had developed and mastered a very delicate kind of microsurgery, a way of excising non-invasive cancerous growths from one's vocal cords. This was a highly specialized surgical technique; it allowed him to remove the most minimal sections of the impacted cord in the hope of leaving "negative margins," a term that means only healthy tissue remains, and that area on the cord is "clear" of any cancer cells.

Of course I hoped for the best results, but after the first pass "under the knife" I learned the margins were still positive. I was scheduled for another round of surgery.

Without being too graphic, let me just tell you that this surgical technique required a procedure that—afterward—felt to me like an entire army of doctors had walked down my throat wearing hiking boots. For several days swallowing was impossible and, of course, I was told not to speak a single word. The thought of repeating this experience was traumatic in and of itself, not to mention having to endure another procedure. But what could I do? I did not want radiation, or to go through chemo, so back into the operating theater I went. The post-operative painful effects were, as you might imagine, double what they were the first time.

To make a long story "short," it was five months and six operations later that I awoke in the hospital recovery room, coming back into my body and experiencing the first awareness of a pain that was now amplified by what felt to be a hundredfold.

My mind, still groggy from the powerful anesthesia that was used to put me to sleep, began to talk to me in negative images, projecting an endless series of surgeries to follow this last one. But it was my body that was doing most of the "talking." It was telling me, in no uncertain terms, that it could not endure one more ounce of pain. It wasn't a threat; this was a cry from the depths of some part of me that felt like it had come to the end of its capacity to suffer. A wave of self-pity washed through me such as I had never known and, as painful as it was to my throat, my body and I began to quietly sob.

At that point, as best I can remember, the recovery room nurse came over, helped set me up a bit in the bed, and put an ice chip in my mouth to alleviate the dryness and help cool the inflamed tissues. And that's when something happened that literally changed my life; it's the whole reason why I'm telling you this story.

As I looked around the stark cancer ward surgery recovery room, I could see someone else was sitting up in a bed just across from me. She was thin and elderly, and had obviously been there during whatever time it took me to return to consciousness. As my eyes shook off the veiling effect of the drugs in my body, and became better adapted to the light in the room, I could see that sitting next to her—holding and gently stroking her outstretched hand—was an equally elderly man. I thought to myself this must be her husband. Then I turned my attention back to get a better look at the woman, who must have come out of surgery just before I did.

To be honest, I don't know if it was the lingering effect of the anesthesia, or that something in me just didn't want to really look at her, but I do remember the impulse to avert my eyes when she finally came into focus. Like myself, she had been operated on to remove whatever malignancy had co-opted her body. But whatever the surgeon had opted to do, obviously to try and save her life, required the removal of most of her jaw. I knew this to be true not because of what I could see, but rather by the absence of familiar facial features that were just no longer there beneath the bandages.

Under normal circumstances, I think I would have looked away from her. For one thing, I didn't want to be rude, to make her more uncomfortable than she already was.

But, as I continued looking at her, I could feel something began to collect in me. It was a kind of quiet conviction that, as best I can express, felt like this: rather than avoid these difficult impressions I was receiving, I should delve deeper into them. And even though it felt contradictory to my usual wish to avoid seeing anything—or anyone—in such a state of distress, I obeyed the intuition. I'm so glad I did. The whole event, my state of being, the room, the smells, her face, every last unwanted part of how I felt—all and everything coalesced into a series of moments and actions whose effects still linger today. Here's what happened next, as best I am able to tell it.

As I looked at her, I was struck by a number of soul-shaking realizations at once—something like what happens as a wave builds and crests, suddenly releasing all of its pent-up powers into a single movement that rushes forward without restraint.

First, I could see, *feel* that she was in an extraordinary amount of pain; and further, that this intense suffering was more than just physical. She knew she had been disfigured by the operation, and I have no doubt that part of her suffering included the pain—still to come—of knowing that people would never be able to look at her in the same way. But what really caught my attention in this moment was the fact that she seemed more concerned about her husband's pain and confusion than her own. It was as if she knew that he was stroking her hand more to console himself than to bring comfort to her.

So overwhelming was this whole impression, so taken was I by her obvious act of compassion that somehow allowed her to put his pain before her own, that I didn't even notice a massive change that had taken place in me.

My pain, all of my self-centered concerns that had consumed me mere seconds before, all of it…had just vanished; gone, like it was never there, even though I was still aware of the conditions that had created it, and that were still in place.

As best I can state it, in some unspeakable manner I knew that whatever the extent of my pain, it was as nothing compared to what this woman and her husband were being asked to endure in that same moment. Not only did this awareness of their suffering serve, in some strange way, to lift me out of my own, but before I knew it, I was moved to get out of my bed, albeit a little uncertain in my steps, and walk over to them. I wanted to tell them something that I had come to know in just that moment, a single thought that I knew was true.

They both looked at me as I approached her bed, and it was clear that they were wondering what on earth was this strange man, in his flimsy hospital gown, doing out of his recuperating cubical. I smiled at them. And when I was close enough for them to hear me—knowing that I was about to do just what I had been told I must not do—I whispered these words, as best I was able to speak them:

"Everything is going to be all right."

Ever so slightly, she managed to nod back at me in agreement; his eyes said, "thank you." And so there we were, the three of us—each in a pain all our own—yet none of us felt alone or overwhelmed. Whatever hurting each of us had been in the moment before had been turned into a wish to help one another through that storm.

We sat there together, in a silent but shared understanding, until a few moments later when the nurse came and scolded me for getting out of my bed unattended.

I couldn't speak it, but if I could, I would have told her that I didn't walk across the room by myself. Love helped me help this elderly couple, and in so doing, I too was helped, not only to transcend my own unwanted state, but I was also helped to see, to understand a lesson in love that I will never, ever forget:

In that most rare of moments shared between us we were no longer a set of strangers—three people suffering by themselves in that recovery room. Something greater than the sum of the parts had come and replaced our pain with an uncompromised compassion. An order of love I hadn't even known existed had brought a healing to us all.

Helpful Questions and Answers

Question: I know I'm too "quick on the draw" when it comes to those moments where my husband does something to displease me, and I'd like to stop punishing him for what—as often as not—is likely *my* mistaken perception of his actions. I don't really like this part of myself, and I'm sure my husband feels the same way. Any suggestions would help!

Answer: The following prescription can be "bitter" at first, but try it and see if it doesn't help empower you to detect and then drop these kinds of negative reactions: The next time you get ready to let some sarcastic or unkind remark fly out of your mouth—taste it, yourself... *before* you dish it out.

Question: I was always under the impression that love and hatred are kind of natural opposites; you know... like they come together in the same package. But I'm getting the impression here that there are different kinds of love, and that the one you're talking about here must be different somehow. Can you help me understand this distinction, if there is one?

Answer: The great majority of all the relationships we've ever seen and known are—as you suggest—built on a love born of the opposites. At this level, love is a kind of shapeshifter: it can turn on a dime into something dark or "unloving" the moment it meets any condition that challenges its fragile place in our heart. But, to the point, your intuition here is right.

Love, as is true of all heavenly forces, *is in levels*, and the kind of love referred to in this book is of a higher order; that is to say, it is not the opposite of hate, any more than light is the opposite of the shadow it casts.

To put this last idea into perspective, fighting with our partner over who's right and who's wrong doesn't prove "how far" we're willing to go for the sake of love. What it does prove is just how far away we are in that moment from the love that brought us together. *The only way any resentment or anger can remain between us and our partner is in the absence of love.* The more we will work with each other to remember this simple truth, the more love will work—for us—to help reveal, and then heal, whatever misunderstanding may have come between us.

KEY LESSONS

1. We are not meant to keep accounts with others, to fill ourselves with blame about where they failed to meet our demands. Nor are we created to carry around with us the cruel and careless remarks of others, and this includes our regrets for where we may have done the same. We can learn to exchange this nature of resentment, that lives to revisit disappointments, with a new and higher understanding that can no more feel punished by the sleeping actions of others than does a mountain feel pain in the midst of a thunder storm.

2. Blaming conflict-filled feelings, or any painful negative state, on the actions of our partner is like getting angry at our shoes for being laced too tight!

3. Real compassion lies in our ability to remember that any time we witness our partner expressing a negative state like anger or resentment, what we're actually seeing in that moment is a loved one who can no longer bear the weary weight of his or her own carefully concealed despair.

8

The Awakening of a Selfless Love
That Encompasses All

Most of us have probably come across, or at least heard mentioned in some way, the iconic idea that *"perfect love casts out fear."*

These five words are ascribed to Saint John in the Gospels, but it is not this attribution that makes them ring true, or that allows us to understand their meaning without having to think too much about it.

There is in each of us a corresponding part to whatever is timelessly true. Something in our mind effortlessly resonates with these ideals. Some part of our heart is lifted in their presence. And while this book isn't the right place to present them all, there are found in holy writings—east and west—many thoughts similar to this last idea that in the light of higher love, no dark fear may dwell. But, as I hoped to illustrate by telling you my personal story in the last chapter, casting out fear and its despair is only *one* of love's powers.

We're about to discover how this higher order of love can also help us cast off the pain, resentment, regret, or any other kind of suffering we may be going through with our partner. The simple teaching story that follows will help illustrate, clarify, and summarize the principles we've examined up to this point.

A middle-aged man had recently moved into a new city and, soon after, decided that he wanted to explore his immediate area, maybe meet some of his neighbors, as well as visit some of the interesting shops that lined the streets all around his apartment.

Less than half an hour later, not knowing the lay of the land, he accidentally walked into an adjacent neighborhood whose streets had been long since "claimed" by an infamous gang. As he realized his situation, and tried to find the fastest way back to relative safety, he made another mistake: looking for the quickest way home, he cut through an alley where a heartless band of thugs beat and robbed him. Summoning all his strength, he dragged himself out from behind a dumpster where they had left him, and crawled just to the entrance of the alleyway where his faint cries for help were all but drowned out by the roar of passing traffic.

Dozens of people walked by him as he lay there. Their eyes were open, but blind to anything other than where they were going and what had to be done when they got there. The first person to walk by the alleyway and take notice of this poor man lying there was the wife of a local city councilman.

She was dressed in the latest spandex workout gear, on her way to the nearby park to do her daily power walk. So involved was she in her own thoughts about a pending dinner party for some VIPs that she had almost walked past the alley before she realized someone was lying there—on the ground—and in obvious pain.

But no sooner did the impression of his misfortune pass through her mind then came this parallel thought: not only was his particular situation none of her business, but it might prove dangerous if she got involved. After all, who knew what might still be lurking there in the shadows. Besides, she was already behind schedule for that day. And so she kept walking ahead, troubled by her own decision until she stopped to chat with a friend she saw sitting in the window of her favorite coffee shop.

Several minutes more passed when came walking down the same street, only headed in the opposite direction, a man wearing new blue jeans that cost him extra money for their used, torn, and soiled look. His open leather sandals showed off a pedicure he'd just received from a nearby salon.

He was the owner-operator of the area's largest franchised health food store, on his way to meet and greet a well-known spiritual author scheduled to appear there in less than thirty minutes. He knew he was late, and hoped that his store manager had seen to the comfort of both the author and the select group of individuals he'd invited to attend the special presentation.

Almost as soon as he saw the beaten man lying there he took a few steps toward him, but was soon stopped cold by one of his own thoughts: it wasn't as if he didn't want to help, but there was much to be considered. One mustn't act too hastily when recent stories abounded of injured people who turned around and sued those who tried to help them. And so, looking around to ensure no one saw him leaving the scene, he decided better to be safe than sorry. As he headed toward his store he made a mental note to notify the authorities as he soon as he got there.

Less than five minutes later, another woman came walking by this man who was still lying there, slipping in and out of consciousness. Surmising his state in an instant, she immediately took off her jacket, folded it into a pillow, and slipped it under the man's bruised head to lift it off the dirty asphalt. Several thoughts were running through her mind all at the same time. She could call 911 but knew, given the deteriorating conditions in resources and response time, it might be thirty minutes before someone got there to render aid; and he was wounded and looked like he needed immediate help.

What if trying to move him made things worse, not to mention possible litigation should things go wrong?

A moment later she ran to where she had parked her car, pulled it alongside the beaten man, and managed to pull him into the back seat. Less than five minutes later, paramedics at the local hospital had the man on a gurney, and she was standing before the receiving desk being asked a host of questions by the nurse on duty:

"Who's responsible for this man? He has no wallet, no identification, let alone any kind of insurance card; who's going to pay for the emergency services he needs?"

"Please, just look after him; attend to his needs. I will cover the expenses that have to be considered until he comes to, and then we can sort out the rest of these details, as needed."

"If you don't mind me saying so, you must be one very compassionate person to get him here, admitted, and receiving care … all the while not knowing if he's covered, or if state programs will provide for his services."

"Oh no, nothing like that, believe me. Truth be told, when I saw this man the thought came to me—more than once—to look the other way."

"Then why, if you don't mind telling me, go through all the trouble … knowing how much could go wrong for you trying to do what was right?"

"Seeing him lying there, knowing he wasn't able to help himself, stirred a part of me I didn't even know I had; it's hard to explain, really, but in that moment, not only did I see the pain he was in but, for some reason, *I felt it as if it were my own.* And that was it; I could no more ignore his suffering in that moment than I would be able to ignore my own.

She paused for a moment to see if the nurse understood what she was trying to convey. And when the nurse nodded her head, she finished her thought:

"So, are we all good to go here? Is everything in place as needs to be to make sure he's cared for?"

"Yes, ma'am, everything is fine. And may I say what a pleasure it is to meet someone like you."

"The same to you…and I'll check back with you in a little while, to see how he's doing."

Learn to Open the "Eyes" of Your Heart and Let the Real Healing Start

We will now reveal, psychologically speaking, the somewhat shocking "true identity" of this unfortunate man who had been beaten, robbed, and left in pain: *this person is me; he is you*; and much to the point of the story, "he" is everyone we know…*including our partner.*

I know this idea comes as a surprise to most of us, but the wise ones who have gone before us in search of unconditional love have long understood this truth. Here's how the great American Poet Laureate, Henry Wadsworth Longfellow, conveys this same precious lesson:

"If we could read the secret history of our enemies, we should find in each man's life sorrow and suffering enough to disarm all hostility." [6]

In other words, and intimately related to the subject at hand: if we could be aware of the pain that our partner—our temporary "foe" in a heated moment—carries in their heart, then *all* attempts to prove them wrong—let alone want to punish them for it—would end on the spot.

For now, please "prove" the following three insights true by looking at them through the eyes of your own past experience. Each and all help make it clear why, at some point in time, you, me, and everyone we know—including our partner—has been the "unfortunate man" in our story.

1. One way or another, all of us have felt ourselves take a "beating" upon finding out that we'd been betrayed, lied to, or cheated by someone we had given our trust.

2. We know what it's like to feel "robbed" any time our partner fails to fulfill one or more of our expectations, or "steals" our joy with an uncaring word or deed.

3. Ninety-nine percent of us have had our heart broken, *more than once*. This kind of pain, the fear of it—with all of its "baggage"—seeps in and colors every relationship that follows, whether we're aware of its presence or not.

---

6. *The Prose Works of Henry Wadsworth Longfellow: Complete in Two Volumes* (Boston: Ticknor and Fields, 1857).

We also know that even though we may have found ways to mask the major portion of this pain, that *doesn't* mean we don't carry it with us. It may be "out of sight," but we know it's never left our mind any time our partner pushes whatever may be our "button" in that particular moment.

These last few insights, and the lessons taken from my personal account as illustrated in the parable that followed, lead us to a story far greater than the sum of its parts. Taken all together, they point to a singular revelation with the power to start a healing process not just with our partner, but also with everyone we know. Let's review these important findings.

Whenever we're filled with blame, unable to see anything but one side, "our side," of the story...

...Anytime all we can hear is some part of ourselves "telling" us why our partner must pay for our pain...

...In these, and in any moment where we find ourselves set against the one we love, we have been rendered effectively blind to a bigger story that we can't see, even though it's right before our eyes: the pain in these moments isn't just mine, and neither is it just yours; *it exists as it does because—one way or another—we're (in it) together; which means...it is* ours.

If we could become conscious of this invisible similarity, be aware of how our partner suffers just as we do— even though their suffering may name itself differently than does ours in that moment—then we could no longer be played against one another.

We'd be unable to say hurtful, heartless things, or take some unkind, thoughtless stand. In this awareness of our secret similarity not only is it given to us to know some measure of our partner's pain but, because of this higher relationship, we could no more wish them more of that suffering than we would wish it upon ourselves.

I know that these last ideas are a lot to take in, especially given what is likely, for many of us, a history with partners past or present replete with unresolved bitterness. So, it's more than possible at this point that you may be thinking something like:

"You've got to be kidding! I can barely deal with the pain I'm already in, especially in the throes of some familiar argument with my partner. So, why on earth would I want to realize, let alone share, a measure of their suffering?"

The answer is as beautifully simple as it is remarkable for its compassion: anytime we know someone else is suffering, and have some awareness of that pain as being the same as our own—we cannot add to it.

Love won't let us.

This power of being unconditionally kind toward those who unconsciously hurt us is just *one* of the gifts of higher love. In a way, it gives our heart "eyes" that can see what they were blind to before.

For example, by its light we're able to see that the needs of our partner are really the same as our own, an insight that makes it impossible to mistake their pain as being somehow less important than our own. So that now when our partner dumps on us a pain they don't know what to do with—demanding we pay for a suffering they only know to blame on us—we're able to do what before would have been impossible:

Without any outward announcement to mark this moment, instead of being dragged into some too-familiar fight, we say, silently, to our partner the healing words we learned earlier: "This one is on me."

We agree to make this sacrifice because we've seen that our partner can't yet understand, let alone know, how to use this pain that only exists between us. *So, for the sake of a love that's greater than the both of u*s, we consciously refuse to say or to do a single thing to make their pain worse. It's not because we're somehow better, superior to our partner. We know better than that now. It's because there is a higher power at work here—an order of love that is incapable of being unkind, even to someone who may have hurt us. And it makes possible a kind of sacrifice of one's self that ego can't conceive, let alone find the will to enact.

This is an act of unconditional love. It is true relationship magic.

Three New Intentions
That Give Birth to a Perfect Action of Love

We are learning about a kind of divine, celestial design directed by a conscious order of love that not only underpins all of our relationships, but whose purpose it is to help us perfect them. We've also looked at some of the ways our awareness of this power can open the door to exploring new possibilities with our partner beyond anything we may have imagined before.

Yet, as honorable as it may be to appreciate, or even outwardly profess the reality of this timeless compassionate intelligence, it's not enough by itself. To acknowledge the existence of this higher order of love—*without taking the steps to act on that knowledge*—is like thinking of ourselves as being a daring explorer simply because we read every issue of *National Geographic*!

There is a great law: to whatever extent we're able to see—and to some extent understand—the truth of these principles, so are we "charged" with a responsibility to act as their instrument. Scripture east and west spells out this "duty," as briefly quoted in this short passage from the New Testament: *"For unto whomsoever much is given, of him shall be much required."* [7]

In other words, much is asked of those given "eyes to see" that our individual relationships are part of a *much*

---

7. Luke 12:48, *The Holy Bible*, King James version.

bigger picture; that love has a grand "plan" in place, being played out on innumerable stages, where each of us seems "magically" drawn to another who becomes our partner for as long as that dance of energies allows. And all for a single purpose: *to help each other learn how to love one another…perfectly.*

There can be no doubt as to the beauty and the promise inherent in these timeless ideas. But, of themselves, beauty and promise are not enough. Yes, they are a reflection of love, but not the same as its "hands on" power—an all-encompassing compassion born of realizing that our partner's pain is the same as our own.

Before we can know this new kind of healing—born of seeing it's impossible to make our partner "sorry" for whatever they did without increasing the measure of our own sorrow—there is something we must *do*.

Nelson Mandela, the self-sacrificing activist who helped end apartheid in South Africa, tells us why it's time to put away "childish things" such as simply hoping that "tomorrow" will change the pain we repeat with our partner today: *"Action without vision is only passing time, vision without action is merely daydreaming, but vision with action can change the world."*[8]

All of that is to say, whether our dream is to share unconditional love with our partner or to be a more kind

---

8. Mandela, Nelson, "50 Inspirational Nelson Mandela Quotes That Will Change Your Life," AwakentheGreatnessWithin.com (accessed 2017).

and compassionate human being, *we must begin to act* on that wish...unconditionally. So, with this idea in mind, let's gather the higher self-knowledge we've gained to date, and turn it into a set of three higher intentions that serve a single purpose: *to help us learn how to love our partner as we wish to be loved by them.*

NEW INTENTION #1

The moment you feel yourself getting all "heated" up—whether a thought has come along to remind you of some unresolved problem with your partner, or because your partner actually does something that causes you to feel upset...stop right there. Give no further thought to any part of yourself *that wants to justify your right to feel wrong.* Do this instead: stop "thinking" and *start seeing that something (negative) has been stirred in you that demands you make your partner pay for your distress.*

NEW INTENTION #2

Remaining present to the heightened self-awareness that your conscious pause helps create, see the truth of the following: the more you identify with these unconscious negative states—and all of the reasons *they* give you to resent, or otherwise oppose, some characteristic in your partner—*the easier it is to set yourself against the one you love.*

New Intention #3

Rather than allow unconscious parts of yourself to re-member negative reasons why you have the right to be resentful—or how much your partner "owes" you for all you've endured on their account—do this: the moment you sense yourself being set against the one you love, ask yourself this one simple question, however you wish to frame it at the time:

Is it possible to really love someone and want to hurt them at the same time? And along these same lines: *Can I ever hope to understand the pain that moves my partner to act against me, if all I want to do in these same moments is inflict a similar pain on them?*

We know the true answer to these questions; or, that is, we should: real love and resentment, compassion and unkindness, can't occupy the same place at the same time.

What this means is that you and I must decide which of these characteristics will occupy our heart in the moment of question. It is a choice that only we can—and must—make even if our partner never knows the kind of sacrifice it entails.

Please note that the following calls for a *completely new kind of action* on our part. More importantly, that it calls for a work to be carried out in our heart anytime we feel hurt and want to blame our partner for that pain.

For the sake of brevity and clarity, I'll restate this third intention in the form of an affirmation, as if addressed to our partner. And while these words and what they express are not something we would ever choose to speak out loud, the responsibility to enact their intention is ours alone.

"My partner: I know you can't see what you're like right now, let alone how your actions are hurting me. And while you may have no awareness of my pain, it has brought me into an acute awareness of yours. So even though I can hear and feel a hundred different 'voices' within me, each demanding 'an eye for an eye'—love will not allow me to add a single measure of more pain to your life than I know you are already in."

How to Invoke Love's Divine Magic

Let's examine one last "real-time" example—an up-close-and-personal look at how this new intention could play itself out as we might practice it—in real time—with our partner.

Imagine that we're out to dinner, driving in a car somewhere, or maybe just lying in bed moments before it's time to turn out the lights. All is well. Everything seems quiet. Then, seemingly out of nowhere, our partner tosses a "grenade" into our lap.

Suddenly, but too late, it's obvious: we didn't see any of the familiar signs that usually indicate a conflict is about to erupt. Perhaps they say something overtly cruel, or make some passive aggressive comment to remind us where we went wrong earlier that evening, or maybe even five years ago.

Almost instantly, from out of our mouth comes pouring a host of tried and true things we tend to say in similar situations; words with edges to cut, some smooth enough to defuse the situation, others more forceful, and all designed to turn the tide of battle and push our partner back onto their heels.

But then, a shift; something within us remembers that we've been where this fight is about to take us at least a hundred times, and that there's nothing new or good about getting there; just more of the same.

In that same revelation, in fact as a part of its remembrance, we now see what we couldn't before: we're about to wade into a "war" with our partner that can't be won no matter which of us seems to come out on top! And so, given what this new level of higher awareness shows us as being true, there's the only logical, and ultimately loving, action left for us to do: *we refuse the call to combat.*

Instead of going ballistic, we go inwardly quiet.

But let us tread this new path carefully: we are *not* surrendering ourselves to the misguided will or whims of our partner. We've seen how that path leads only to resentment when, as it must happen, we can no longer bear the brunt of being in such an inequitable relationship. The real question before us, given we can see the truth of our situation, is this: what difference does it really make which of us seems to be "steering" our canoe *when we're both headed for the falls*! One of us has to wake up and change course, even if our partner is unable, or even unwilling, to see the wisdom of that choice at the time we make it. And that's why we don't engage as an "enemy" someone that we loved only moments before.

Instead, we deliberately drop the false assumption that coercing our partner to pay for our pain can do anything other than increase whatever resentment may be growing between us.

Neither do we allow this bitterness to "think" for us, so that not only do we detect and reject its conclusions as our own, but we also refuse to lend it use of our voice to speak *its* demands, without which there is no fight.

In short, *we give ourselves up*.

We surrender ... but *not* to our partner.

Instead we take the one path that remains open to us, given what our new understanding about higher love has shown us is true. Having seen that we remain powerless to drop our own unconscious demands, and how—much in the same way—our partner is equally unable to do anything other than insist we make the "payment due" for their pain, we are left with no other option:

We agree to "die" to any parts of ourself we can feel trying to push us, in any way, to identify with and then enact *their* old solutions. Rather than uselessly suffer some well-worn pain that our lower nature usually blames on our partner, we choose to drop not only it, but also *any familiar sense of ourselves that may be connected to it* as well.

In other words, *we agree to voluntarily suffer the death of this false self* that love has shown us knows not what it does to us, let alone to those we want least to hurt.

Making this intention—and striving to enact it, as a life-long practice with our partner—*is doing our part* in realizing unconditional love. In truth, it's really the only thing that is in our power to do. Which brings us to this closing promise:

If we will do our part, love will do the rest; but we must put it to the test.

Embrace these new ideas. Enact them. Let them prove love's power to heal and perfect all who will dare invoke its divine magic.

Helpful Questions and Answers

Question: It's not like he means it, but somehow my partner *knows* how to push the wrong button in me, and always at exactly the wrong time. It's as if he waits for me to say yes, to something, so that then he can say no. So, while I'd really like to learn how to be more patient with him than I am, I don't have a clue where to begin. Any hints are greatly appreciated!

Answer: No doubt it's challenging to deal with anyone, let alone a loved one, who contradicts us at every turn. But becoming impatient with his unconscious actions—and then blaming him for them—is like yelling at a toaster to stop burning your bread! The real solution to this, and to all similar situations, *rests within you*, not with your partner. We can only bear some negative characteristic in someone else that we have learned to consciously bear in ourselves... which means none of us can be truly compassionate until we know what it means to suffer for the sake of something greater than ourselves: unconditional love.

Question: I like many of the ideas in this book; most of them resonate with me as true. But honestly... it feels like you're asking for more than I'm able to give when it comes to letting go and letting love lead me through the trials that I face almost every day with my partner. I want to believe in higher love—to be able to act with the kind of compassion you've called out here as not just our possibility, but our responsibility, as well. Please tell me how I can begin to see this power, so that I might build a greater trust in it.

Answer: We must not just "believe" in the power of love; billions profess this belief, and yet... billions still hurt one another in the name of love. We must learn to see—with our "new eyes"—that love is within and around us at all times. For instance, here's an example of something that's always been right before us, as a fact of life, but that has remained just out of sight (until today)! The love we have for anything holy, beautiful, or true is present in our heart before we can think of any reason for the love that we feel. The breathtaking light at sunset, that strain of delicate music, or watching a mother tenderly embrace her child: these moments don't create the love we feel for what we see before us; these moments reveal the presence, and the power, of a love that already lives within us! Do take a moment to consider all that this insight implies, including one of the main themes of this whole book: it isn't we who find things to love, but rather that Love finds—through us—a way to reach us, and to teach us that She lives in and through all things…including us.

KEY LESSONS

1. The reason it's pointless to ask, or otherwise demand, that anyone in our life explain themselves to us—for what amounts to our troubled feelings over their words or actions—is because no one in the world can explain away a pain that we're creating for ourselves!

2. For real love to survive and thrive between you and your partner in life, you're going to have to discover another kind of love that isn't divided up into who's right and who's wrong. It's that simple, because as long as you have someone, anyone, to be against, you cannot be for love.

3. While it may feel, at times, as if fighting with your partner is in your best interests because it seems certain that such suffering is in *love's* best interest, nothing is further from the truth. It isn't for the sake of love that you fight. *It can't be...* that is, unless you believe that the way to build a house is to tear down its walls. And now, more to the point at hand: *it's not really "you"* who wants to start, let alone stoke the flames that give rise to these fights. *It is this false sense of self*—born of identifying with one side or the other of the unconscious opposing forces that make it feel real—*that must be surrendered.*

9

Start Making Space
for Your Partner to Grow

It was a little before seven a.m. on Saturday morning when Alex sat down in his living room with his first cup of coffee. He was up a little bit earlier than usual because a strange noise had awakened him from his sleep. So, when he looked out of his bedroom, he wasn't too surprised to discover the source of the disturbance was his neighbor Sam, who lived just across the street. Sam was dragging several folding tables out of his garage, and arranging them on the front lawn. From the look of things, including a couple of stacks of cardboard boxes, it appeared that Sam was setting the stage for a household rummage sale.

Partly out of curiosity, and partly out of irritation—wanting to see why on earth Sam felt the need to get such an early start—Alex threw his robe over his PJs and walked over to where Sam was arranging the things he intended to sell. As he made his way across the street, he could see his breath forming mini-clouds in the air. It was late spring, but there was a chill still rolling off the snow-capped mountains that surrounded their valley homes.

"Good morning, Sam," said Alex. "My, but aren't you out here bright and early!"

Apparently Sam didn't hear the hint of sarcasm in Alex's voice; either that or he just didn't care...which irritated Alex a little bit more.

"Good morning to you," said Sam, wearing a warm smile on his face. "Looks to be a nice day, doesn't it?"

But now it was Alex who didn't hear what Sam had said, because his attention was captured by something he never thought he would see for sale, let alone in a front yard rummage sale. It was Sam's set of favorite paintings that had taken a great many years to collect. But there, spread out over several tables, sat about a dozen different signed renditions of the Rocky Mountains. Each one featured a different scene, highlighting the natural majesty that surrounded the valley where they lived. A famous naturalist had painted them all, and they were highly collectible.

Alex was stunned. Several thoughts raced through his mind at the same time: Why would Sam want to sell what had to be one of his most prized possessions? Could he be in some kind of financial trouble? Was he ill?

The next moment, before he even knew that his mouth had formulated the words, Alex blurted out:

"I'm not prying, but what's going on, man?" And then, pointing directly at the set of tables where Sam had carefully displayed the art, he continued to ask, "Why on earth are you selling your collection of favorite paintings?"

"Oh, that?" Sam replied, laughing a little as if it was nothing. "I really don't have a choice..."

Alex took a deep breath and said, "Geez, man, can you use a little extra cash, you know, to tide you and the family over...until things get better?"

Realizing now that his friend had misunderstood the situation, Sam set down the dishes he was arranging on the table. "I guess I wasn't as clear as I should have been. What I really meant when I said 'I don't have a choice' is that *I want to sell it*."

Looking at Alex's reaction, and seeing that he still didn't understand what was going on, Sam continued.

"Look, it's simple: I'm selling my set of paintings because I need to make space in my living room for something a lot more valuable to me."

Still confused, Alex asked, "What are you talking about, Sam?"

"Just come with me into the house for a moment, okay? Let me show you something that should make the whole thing clear."

A moment later, Sam and Alex stood before the now bare south wall of the living room where Sam's collection of art had been hanging only hours ago. But, before he had a chance to explain his plan, Alex asked him:

"Okay, I get it. You're going to hang something else on this wall. But what could you possibly put here that would give you as much pleasure as the paintings you just took down?"

Sam answered Alex with a question of his own: "Do you know what's on the other side of this wall?"

Not at all sure what was being asked of him, Alex shook his head as if to say, "Why no, Sam...no, I don't."

With that, Sam turned toward the wall, his eyes wide and full of expectation. He stood there for a moment, almost as if he was looking past it, taking in a sight only he could see.

"Yes, you do, Alex. Just think about it for a second, and I'm sure you'll see what I do."

"What are you about...see what?"

"The Rocky Mountains, man, stretched out as far as the eye can see! *That's* what's on the other side of this wall."

"I...I still don't get it."

"I'm going to remove most of this whole wall...and replace it with one giant picture window. *Now* do you understand why I'm selling my collection? I want to raise some money for the renovation."

"Wow...seems like a lot to go through, let alone what you have to give up, don't you think?"

"Maybe, but you know the old saying: 'There's only one way to make room for what's new, and that's out with the old.' Right?"

"Well, I suppose so..."

"No doubt about it. Besides, ask yourself this question: which would you rather wake up to look at every day? Some old paintings of the Rockies from days long gone by, or...a view of *the real majesty* itself?"

Alex looked back at Sam and smiled: "Yeah...okay. *Now* I get it."

Introducing One of the Great Unseen Laws of Higher Love

In this simple story is hidden a deep message that, in one form or another, is found in every true teaching about love as it affects our ability to have, enjoy, and enrich all of our relationships, but especially when it comes to the one we love. Simply put:

Before any order of a new or higher love can enter into our heart, *we must make room for it* by "selling"—deliberately giving up—something that we once held as being of value to us. Let's look at a few simple examples of this law in action.

If we want to exercise, become healthier, we must give something up in order to make it so. Perhaps we make room for our new, more active lifestyle by giving up time on social media, watching TV, or even just sleeping in that extra half-hour in the morning. All of this should be self-evident: without being willing to exchange the former for the latter, one for the other, nothing can come of our wish to get into better shape.

Here's another example. Perhaps something like this happened to you? I remember when I just turned thirteen years old; it was my first go-round with having a "serious" girlfriend. I knew it had to be serious because it caused me to make what felt like a life-changing decision.

At the time, as best I can recall the event, my three best friends sat me down under a tree at the park, saying we had to discuss something about my recent behavior that was "bothering" them.

They went on to tell me I was spending *way* too much time with my new girlfriend, and not enough time running with them, as we had always done. The choice before me was simple, if not painful:

If my wish was to spend more time with my first crush, it meant I had to give up part of a familiar role with my old friends. Not an easy choice, because it was all new territory back then. Of course, my friends eventually came to see the light and to forgive me...but only after they too had to give up something of their old ways to make room in their lives for their first touch of a new love.

Can you see the way this simple but true story validates the lessons we just learned in the last chapter? When it comes to the birth of any new love, but especially with our partner in life, there is a law that governs its arrival: *we have to make room for it.* And further, fulfilling this law always requires that we give up, sacrifice something that we're identified with and attached to…whether that be old images, old pals, or our own old demands.

Start Seeing Your Partner with "New Eyes"

With very few exceptions, the way we look at, and then experience, our interactions with others—but especially when it comes to our partner—is determined by the kind of ideas we bring with us into these relationships.

For instance, maybe our heart got crushed in days gone by; perhaps a loved one betrayed us in a most cruel way, so that now the thoughts we carry with us into each new relationship are pre-colored with a sense of caution we just can't shake. As much as we may wish otherwise, we can't give the whole of our love for fear that our partner may obliterate the little bit of hope and trust that still lives in our heart.

Or perhaps we were in some kind of abusive relationship. It really doesn't matter who may have punished us, or even at what age, be it a past partner or maybe a parent who was maddened with enough pain or frustration to take it out on us.

Nevertheless, what remains are wounds that never seem to heal. When we're given even the slightest hint of having to relive *anything* like the nightmare of our past, our own fearful thoughts rush in to seal us off—stealing from us the possibility of forming a new and meaningful relationship.

This "body" of unconscious thoughts and feelings literally stains our reality, causing us to see our relationships, and their possibilities, through *its* fearful mindset. It doesn't just confine us to live in its dark reality, but it actually helps create this ever-shrinking construct for us by "showing" and "telling" us why—if we don't want to get hurt again—we *need* to be afraid of love! It should be clear: as long as we continue to look at our partner through the "eyes" of these conditioned thoughts and feelings, we have almost no choice but to be a prisoner of the world they see.

This means that we can't really know love's power to free us, to fulfill us through our relationships, until we gain some totally new ideas about how to see, and then interact, with our partner. Not just a rehash of our past failed viewpoint; we know that path is powerless to heal the aching heart. An altogether higher view is called for. We need to be able to see the one we love through the "eyes" of a completely fresh understanding, one that only unconditional love can provide.

To be clear, we are asking: what is the power of love—especially in times of trial with those we love—to not just change *what* we see in difficult moments, but also how we respond to them as well? A simple "real-time" example will help answer this last question.

There are certain moments with our partner that we've all experienced at least a hundred times. Everything is just fine, our love is intact…that is, until our partner acts out some dark mood, expressing—in one way or another—something that we take as being either passively unkind, or obviously aggressive. Then, bang, it's on! We brace ourselves for a collision born of our opposition to whatever we suddenly find to resist in them.

Our perception of these moments is almost instantaneous; we look at our partner as having created a great divide between ourselves and whatever love we may have known only moments before. That's how we see it; which also means *that's how we understand the event*. Now, with no room for doubt as to who is at fault, we know what happens next. One out of any of a hundred old painful patterns is renewed. And not only do both parties involved suffer for its reappearance, but the seeds of that same misunderstanding are sown yet again, virtually ensuring its return at a later time.

Now let's look at this same kind of old, unwanted moment through the "eyes" of the new ideas we've been learning are true when it comes to unconditional love.

We may say, and even believe, that the anger or disappointment we feel toward our partner is because "we love them," but now we can begin to suspect that's just *not* true. After all, how can love ever be the reason why we feel estranged from the one we love? Even common logic can see: real love *never* separates, any more than sunlight divides itself up into light and shadow. Shadows only come into existence when something gets in the way of light, and not because light has been somehow destroyed! The following is beyond doubt: *love never departs those who choose to see their partner in its light.*

Learn to Welcome This Immeasurable Power of Love Into Your Life

Here, where I live, atop a small mountain in southern Oregon, my office and home are surrounded by towering fir, pine, and oak trees. Intermingled among them is a healthy spattering of large madrone trees, decked out with their perennial crown of waxy green leaves.

When the evening breezes come rolling up the incline from the valleys below, as they almost always do right before sunset, the leaves on these trees seem to come alive. Not only are they transformed into millions of tiny sails that catch the waves of wind, but as the trees sway to and fro under their canvas, they create an infinite number of shadows that dance along the ground for as long as the sunlight lends them a temporary life.

Now, as a rule, unless something moves us to look up at the sun, we rarely notice, let alone see, the light that radiates from it.

In some ways, this all-pervasive light from our star is a lot like the projector at the movie theater. Just as we don't see the light that streams out of it, filling the screen before us with moving images, neither do we see the living light that beams down on us, without which we would see none of the forms or colors it brings into our sight, let alone the shadows they cast.

Much as this is true about this light that, itself, we don't see, so is it true when it comes to our health; we don't really "see" it.

For the most part, we're virtually unaware of our own well-being...that is, until something comes along to take it from us! Only then are we made conscious of two things at once: first, we're given an inescapable awareness that a precious balance in our body has been lost. And second, inseparable from this first realization, an understanding that if we're to restore our health, we must do whatever it takes to atone for its loss.

Keeping these last two examples in mind—of how we live in a light that we see only because of the world it reveals to us, plus the fact that our health itself is unseen by us until it goes "missing"—let's look at the equally invisible, but absolutely critical, role that *love* plays in our relationships.

For starters, love instantly "feels" the appearance of any disparate force that comes along to upset the sensitive balance between us and the one we love; as such, our ability to sense the entrance of that negative influence often allows us to drop its disturbance before it sets us apart. But *that's just a small part of love's power.* The light of this same delicate awareness serves another purpose: it reveals, silently, the *real* nature of whatever is responsible for this sudden loss. The two examples that follow will help shed some valuable light on this last important idea:

Where *we see* someone to blame for failing to meet our expectations, *love sees* that there could be no such resentment without our having identified with an unconscious part of ourself that believes its demand should be the same as their command.

Where *we see* someone to resent for not giving us the approval we want from them, *love sees* that this pain belongs to an unconscious nature that believes it's only as worthwhile as the number of smiles it can win, and further, that this insatiable level of self can never win enough.

And yet, for all of love's inestimable power to feel, and then reveal, the parts of ourself that stand in the way of its healing...it is powerless to work this kind of relationship magic without our consent. How could it be otherwise? After all, even though love may be the greatest force in all of creation, it never forces itself on anyone.

Enter Into a Full Partnership With Love

Love often appears at our door as a beggar in disguise. There are countless ancient myths that tell how the gods would show up at the door of someone's home, appearing to be in dire straits. On the surface of things, they seem to be seeking food and shelter; but, in truth, they've come to ask if the ones they have chosen to visit will make room for them in their lives. And, as these stories go, whoever agrees to make this kind of sacrifice—for the sake of their unexpected visitors—is rewarded by them beyond their wildest dreams.

In much the same way, love is always knocking on our door. But it never does so more stridently than when our heart closes itself off to our partner in the name of some unconscious pain that we blame on them.

In unhappy moments like these, not only do we slam the door shut in the face of the one we love but, without ever knowing it, we also deny ourselves the precious, timeless gifts that only love can offer us: *a full partnership with all of its powers*. These gifts include the unfailing presence of an unconditional compassion for all that it embraces. This level of higher self-understanding can *never* be pulled into a fight with our partner because it can't be deceived into identifying with one side or another of some unconscious opposing force.

Now, if it's not already clear, the part of us that rejects the offer of such a remarkable power lives on in us largely undetected. This happens because, for the most part, it dwells deep in some unlit region of our consciousness. But we can begin the process of illuminating this lower nature by looking at a few of our own simple memories from days gone by. I'll spell out some of my own recollections, hoping that even if you don't share similar moments, you can relate to them enough for us to arrive at the point they're intended to help make.

When I was still very young, I loved watching TV at night with my parents in their bedroom. Inevitably, I would fall asleep and one of them would pick me up and tote me off to my own room. I can still remember the way it felt to be carried that way, in their arms, and dropping off back to sleep even before I was tucked in for the night.

In later years, there were those most delicious moments when Mom would bake a cake. She would make chocolate frosting using an electric mixer. It had a pair of detachable whisk-like attachments that—when covered with the frosting left clinging to them—my brother and I would get to lick clean.

I loved these gifts that came with growing up and, of course, too many others to mention. All of them were a part of being raised in a home that, for the greatest part, was governed by love. But this isn't to say that being in the hands of love was always so comforting, or welcome. Other memories come from those times as well!

There were many moments, more than I care to recount, that often felt punitive; as bitter as were the better ones sweet. Who can forget being "summoned" to his or her parent's side where you were brought to task for getting into some kind of trouble at school, with friends, or—as was often the case with me—getting into a scrap with my older brother. Where, in spite of all my clever excuses, I was found "guilty" and sentenced for having broken the house rules...some of which I didn't even know existed until I broke them!

In short, I adored all the comforts and pleasures, those natural gifts that come with being loved. On the other hand, I wanted nothing to do with the necessary, often painful corrections that this same love often called for. Talk about instant resistance!

As the years rolled on—at least in my case, as I hope is true for you—I came to see that much of this unwanted guidance—dispensed for the sake of love—proved itself wise. And should this same hindsight hold true for you, then it means...we judged our parents falsely. They were not trying to take the joy out of our lives. What they "wanted" from us...*was to give us something that we just couldn't see we needed at that time*: a measure of their hard-won wisdom, including the hope that we might understand it enough to spare us some of the troubles and tears they used to pay for it. And while I don't want to lose sight of the lesson here, I feel I must address the proverbial "elephant" in the room.

It's clear, after decades of meeting and teaching aspirants about the nature of unconditional love—and hearing their stories about the abuse they received from their parents—not all of us look back at our early years with tender thoughts, or with any warm feelings in our heart.

For many of us, there's nothing but regret, or some kind of guilt—a loathing of misused authority; fear and resentment for the harm done to us by cruel or otherwise unconscionable people that we could not escape. So, this unfortunate fact must also be addressed. But, and I leave this to you, the reader, to whom this same kind of pain may apply:

Anyone who abused you—not just as a child, but specifically so in this instance—acted out what he or she did for one reason only: *they did not know what else to do with their pain* other than try to escape it by heaping it on those who couldn't fight back. If you can see this is so, even suspect its truth after having realized some of the same kind of pain in yourself—and felt what it's compelled you to do against others, and yourself—then this new self-understanding…is the beginning of true forgiveness. This compassion is one of the greater gifts of unconditional love.

Now, back to the central theme of this chapter section. While growing up, our tendency was to meet much of the guidance offered to us with resistance, if not out-and-out hostility. And, to remake the point, those who wanted to help guide us through these early days of our journey were not trying to make us unhappy; that was not their wish. We just weren't wise enough to want what they wanted to give us: a small measure of their understanding intended to help us escape some of the pain they didn't.

In very much the same way as illustrated above, so goes our present relationship with some of the gifts that love wants to give us. We just can't recognize them yet...for what they are. Which brings us to this next important insight:

If it's our wish to have and to know unconditional love with our partner, then our relationship can't just be about *what we want—or don't want—from that love we share between us.* If we want the "real deal," then we have to accept *all* of the gifts that come with loving someone, not just the ones that we recognize, or that otherwise seem desirable to us.

Let Go and Help Your Partner Outgrow Their Limitations

Being able to hold one another, make love, share secrets, comfort each other through "thick and thin" moments, explore passions together: these beautiful experiences are all a part of what love makes possible between our partner and us. And yet, as wonderful as these unique gifts may be—that attract us to one another—they have a way of often turning into their not-so-beautiful opposite; where one moment we feel strangely drawn to our partner, and the next we may feel equally repelled, pushed into a place that doesn't feel loving at all. And yet, as we're about to see...

this is exactly the moment when higher love comes knocking at the door, wanting to give us a gift we can't yet see as such. But how can we know that these things are true? The two points that follow should remove any doubt.

1. No one can question that it is the power of love that brings us together with our partner. It is equally obvious that we are *not* the creators of these mysterious forces that draw us to the one we love, any more than a piece of iron and a magnet conspire to create the attraction between them.

2. There can also be no doubt that this same mysterious attraction that brings us together also works to *hold us* together...sometimes even as we're struggling to remember exactly why we came together in the first place!

We're talking about what must be the original "rock and a hard place"!

After all, we did not create this force of attraction between us that, in "right" moments, we wish would only grow stronger and stronger; while, on the other hand, when this feeling flip-flops and turns into its opposite, the *last* person we want to be around is the one we love! And let's not forget those most confusing times when our heart feels both of these things at once!

These conditions that love creates are enough to drive a person "mad" and, in fact, have been known to do just that! After all, why would love draw us into a caring relationship—let us sample its delight—only to dash our hopes by suddenly showing us some unwanted characteristic in our partner that we couldn't see coming?

In strained moments like these, wherein—aided by the light of some unexpected event—we see some unlikable quality in our partner previously hidden from sight, it feels as if our "love boat" has run onto a reef. There's a terrible "sinking" feeling. We feel deceived. The onset of this kind of suffering shouts an alarm: "Abandon ship!"

We should know this pattern by now: the immediate resistance we feel toward our partner not only confirms our negative view of them in that moment but also—as strengthened by this same judgment—proves that we have nothing in us like this disagreeable characteristic that now stands revealed.

But what is it that we're *actually* looking at in our partner? The fact that we want nothing to do with their negative state—whatever its nature—does nothing to change the truth of the following revelation: in these unwanted moments we don't just feel their pain; it's deeper than that. We *know* this suffering as if it's our own.

After all, how else can we explain this acute awareness of what our partner is feeling in these moments if not for the fact that, somehow, we're both experiencing the same thing, at the same time, only from what seem to be separate sides of a single story? Our studies have prepared us to understand the healing answer that follows:

What we are given to see in these moments—what we sense and feel in our partner—is evidence of a wound in their heart that has yet to heal. It is a hurt held over, a pain of some kind that lives on—hidden in them—until something *in that moment of our being together* stirs it awake. But as we've seen, this kind of suffering never stirs by itself, any more than a pebble thrown into a pond could make no ripple; the effect of its awakening in our partner stirs us into the sudden awareness of an equivalent pain that lives in us.

In other words, the pain that we feel in our partner is *a reflection of a corresponding pain that lives in us.* This understanding helps explain why trying to "fix" whatever we see as "broken" in the one we love *always* has to fail. These solutions are as powerless to change how we feel about our partner in that moment … as is trying to cheer ourselves up by looking into a mirror we've just painted with bright "happy" colors!

The importance of this last insight can't be overstated, so let me summarize and restate it: the pain that exists between our partner and us is *not* there to drive us apart. Rather, in a way we can't yet see, this pain that feels like a separating force is more like two pieces of a puzzle waiting to be put together in order to complete one another. If this is true, which it is, then there's really only one thing that's missing in our relationship, keeping us apart: a new understanding that will allow us to see how our seemingly separate parts are really *a single part of a much bigger picture.*

Don't Let This Unseen Pain Turn You Against Your Partner

The next idea may be challenging to some of us, especially if we've had unhappy experiences in our life with people who, for the pain they didn't know what to do with, did nothing but push us away. Nevertheless, it's true: *everything under the sun wants to be loved.*

Let's look at several simple examples of this celestial law: trees reach up to receive the kiss of sunlight that brings them life. Flowers need the touch of the bees that pollinate them. In one way or another, babies of every kind cry out for their parent, wanting to be cared for, nourished, and protected. We can state this same celestial principle using different words:

Everything in existence seeks what it must have, that which alone is created to complete it, and that it exists—in return—to complete.

Nothing is exempt from this law, nothing, and that includes whatever may be the nature of our pain, or the pain of the one we love. Again, everything under the sun seeks what it needs to complete itself, and this includes negative states like anger, resentment, or disappointment.

These negative energies do not come into existence on their own, and neither can they complete themselves—heal themselves—on their own. In other words, no pain is created in our life without there also appearing—in the moment of its conception—what it needs to complete, and to release itself all at once.

Very few people have ever heard the kind of higher ideas such as you are reading here and now, and how they apply to healing our relationships with those we love. These principles belong to a higher level of consciousness that, as it is realized, allows us to see—and to understand—many of the underlying laws that invisibly govern our relationships.

One of these major laws gives us an important insight into some of the unseen forces we're studying in this chapter section, as well as why a true lasting peace with our partner seems so elusive. And while I'm sure that Christ wasn't the first to teach it, the simple way in which he stated this law allows us the most direct access to its wisdom. It should be noted here that, at the time, he was speaking to his disciples, attempting to explain the best way to interact with anyone who would act against them.

He said, and I paraphrase for the sake of brevity: "Resist not evil…but turn your other cheek."

The actual translation of the original Aramaic in which this timeless lesson was first written follows, as extrapolated from *Strong's Concordance with Hebrew and Greek Lexicon:*[9]

> *Do not oppose those who oppose you; [so that] should someone cause you [psychological] pain by striking some vanity [hidden in your nature], wisdom suggests that you don't "demand an eye for an eye." Rather than resist their unwanted action, welcome it; use it to help you better see [realize]— be released from—[a false] lower nature that can't live without having someone or something to be set against.*

This book isn't the right place to examine the teachings of illumined souls—east and west—who lived, in one way or another, to help us learn and grow in the ways of love. Nevertheless, this lesson, simplified and summarized as follows, is one they all taught in common:

As long as we resist—unconsciously oppose—the onset of (any) pain in our partner, we will never be able to see, let alone understand, its real purpose...either in our own life or in that of our partner. Here's the simplest way I know to summarize this law, as well as the action it implies for anyone willing to take it to heart:

---

9. *The New Strong's Expanded Exhaustive Concordance of the Bible* (Nashville, TN: Thomas Nelson, 2010).

For love to grow, anything that opposes it must go…including any old, familiar sense of self that would impose its thoughts on us otherwise.

This last point should be clear enough; yet so many times—especially in times of duress—we lose sight of its perspective and, accordingly, its power to help us remember what matters most. Here's the unseen source of our forgetfulness:

Pain is blind; and because it is…unseeing, it's uncaring.

We know this is true because we've all seen how pain can make us blindly lash out—hurting those we love. And how it's almost always *after* the fact that we regret having turned against our partner, seeing—too late—that some unconscious pain had pushed us into that action. And this door swings both ways: whenever our partner is in pain, they too are blinded by it in every meaning of the word. They can't see what they are doing to themselves, let alone to us.

In a word, we are locked in a true standoff: as long as each of us continues to assume the alternating role of one moment being an irresistible force (i.e., demanding what we're sure our partner "owes" us), and the next moment, an immovable object (i.e., refusing to budge from our insistence that we are the one who is "owed" some kind of payment now due), nothing new can come into this struggle to change it.

Only a greater power, something outside of this pattern, can reveal it and, at the same time, release us from our unconscious role in its continuing creation. All of our studies, insights, and discoveries have prepared us for the answer that follows:

In one respect, this mysterious power isn't really outside of us at all, but rather dwells in the deepest part of our heart. It is a higher level of love that, while it gives rise to the opposing laws of attraction and resistance, is not bound by them. Rather, it transforms these opposing forces into the unity of a new order of awareness in which is revealed not only the possibility of being able to love our partner unconditionally, but also the path that leads us there.

Love's immeasurable gift, for those who will open the door to receive it, is a whole new understanding that changes not just the meaning of *what* we see—and react to—in our partner, but *how* we respond to what our partner reveals to us... *about ourselves.*

Let Love Dissolve the Differences That Divide You From Your Partner

We touched on this same idea in our earlier studies, but now we have a much deeper understanding of it: our relationships, especially with those we love, are a kind of "magic mirror."

Our partner helps bring us into an awareness of qualities and characteristics that otherwise we'd never see as dwelling within us. And we serve the exact same purpose in their life. Further still, whatever level of patience or anger, strength or weakness, cruelty or kindness that any of us have realized in this life, we know each of these qualities within us only because our partner—whoever or whatever that may have been at the time—stirred us into an awareness of it.

Understood properly, this insight means that we are in each other's life as a kind of "secret agent" of this kind of revelation. And as applies to our study, we're all brought together by love for this same reason: so that any pain or limitation still concealed—yet unhealed within us—might be revealed, realized, and integrated into the greater whole of us. Again, a reminder from the second chapter of this book, where Jerry Maguire told his love, Dorothy: "*You complete me.*"

Of course, all of the above sounds great; in fact, perfect! That is until...one of us stirs the proverbial hornet's nest in the other. Suddenly all we see, and know—because our negative reaction tells us so—is that our partner has done us wrong, and what must be done to make things right...again.

But now we know better than to take the side of this resistance that wants to wrap us up in a dark ball and roll us away. Yes, of course our partner may have crossed, and—in fact—will cross, whatever "line" we've drawn in the sand. They *will* test the limits of our patience, kindness, or ability to forgive, as we will theirs.

But, in the light of our recent discoveries, what other circumstances are there that can reveal the parts of us that will only go "so far" for the sake of the one we love?

How else would we ever come to realize the present limits of our capacity to love...so that as grows our willingness to recognize the secret good in these unwanted revelations, so does our ability to see—and to appreciate—our partner for what they are in reality: an "agent" of love whose secret mission is, in part, to initiate the kind of healing that begins with revealing whatever painful characteristic still lives concealed within us.

To whatever degree we sense the healing truth of this last idea, let us also be instructed by it. As the following three examples suggest, now we know *what we can no longer do* whenever our partner does something that brings up a negative reaction in us.

1. We know we must not strike out at our partner in the name of any pain that wants to blame them for its sudden appearance within us.

2. We know we must not strike back at our partner for *our* resistance to whatever negative energy they may be emanating, simply because the only thing this kind of negative reaction does is magnify both of our suffering.

3. We know, as difficult as it may be to remember in the midst of these trials, *we're not there to resist* what we see about our partner, or what they have helped to reveal in us. Instead, *we're there to assist in these revelations* because we understand that no anger, no fear or regret, can heal in us as long as it remains concealed from our awareness of it.

In other words, we have a choice: we can either continue to unconsciously resist this pain that we've always blamed on our partner, standing by, helplessly, as it re-seeds itself again and again, growing into greater levels of frustration, resentment, and mistrust...

...Or we can work to make this resistance, along with its attending pain, *conscious*; we can recognize and realize its appearance in us for what it always has been in reality: the unmistakable awareness of an invitation to let go of who we have been and, at the same time, to grow—along with our partner—into a love that is altogether new, true, and beautiful.

Proof Positive That Changing Your Partner Is Not Your Job

It would never occur to us to point out—let alone to try and change—some part of the one we love unless we weren't first somehow troubled or pained by it.

In other words: whatever those characteristics may be that we set out to "improve" in our partner, it's likely they are the same ones that we most resist in them! This is an important observation to make. Here's why: just about everything we hope to accomplish—to help our partner outgrow whatever it is about them that grates on us—does the opposite of what we set out to do! Let's take a moment and look into what causes this unexpected result.

Anytime we push our partner to change it's because we blame much of our pain in that moment on something in their nature that has set us off, making us negative. So we may say that it's our love for them that's active here, but the real actor behind the scenes, calling the shots, is something about them that we oppose anytime it pops up. Here's the point: while we may see ourselves as "caring" enough to point out their fault, *this is not what our partner feels*. What they feel is the surge of our resistance to them. They react accordingly, and push back.

If we can see what happens once this pattern starts to unfold, then it's clear…the only thing trying to change our partner really accomplishes is to confirm what they've suspected all along: in these moments, *we* are their problem, the source of their pain. But this misperception is only half of the real problem here, and the lesser half at that…

As our partner looks at us as their problem, their mind is crowded with false considerations, and their attending accusations. This flood of negative thoughts and feelings creates a kind of blindness, because there's literally no room left in our partner to see, let alone realize, anything about themselves in that same moment. As a result, it's not that they *won't* work to change, as we might hope, but that they *can't* change ... because they can't see that any change is needed! This last idea is such an important insight that it deserves further explanation, as follows.

If you can recall some telling moment when, for whatever reason, you were able to effect a real change in your nature, was it because someone pushed you to go through that moment? Or was that moment of transformation one and the same as suddenly seeing something about yourself that *you knew you had to change*? Like discovering you were enabling a weakness in someone you love because you'd never seen how deep ran your need for their approval. What you have to do is as clear as day: the only way to help the one you love is to suffer changing yourself. You get the picture.

There's only one way to help our partner grow—to lend them a loving hand in effecting whatever positive changes in their nature they're given to make: we must learn to give them all the room they need to see themselves as they are.

Helpful Questions and Answers

Question: I feel as if I'm stuck in a kind of purgatory. On one hand, I've just entered into a relationship with a wonderful new man, and I want to embrace this opportunity—love him—as fully as I know I'm capable of doing. On the other hand, I'd have never met this man if it weren't for a real jerk crushing my heart just a few months ago. My dilemma is this: I can see I'm afraid to let go and trust my new partner, but I know that if I don't, then our love will have no way to grow. Help!

Answer: Your patient study of the next insight will show you why we must have a new set of eyes to help us see through the lie behind these kinds of fears, as well as the way they mislead us into the very situation we hope to avoid.

When it comes to any form of (psychological) fear... *the "feel" is real, but the "why" is a lie.* In this instance, can you see that whatever fear you feel now—telling you of dark hours to come—doesn't exist without some part of you imagining, revisiting the very past that you hope not to relive? And then, the same unconscious mind, the one responsible for projecting this pain, goes on to tell you how to escape the very fear that *it's* created!

You can't change this painful dream by trying to protect yourself from it, or by trying to control the unwanted moment that it projects. There's only one way to end this kind of nightmare, and that's to shake yourself awake and out of the dream that's causing it.

Question: I've always known that I may be too hard-headed for my own good, and that I'm as responsible for bumping heads with my wife as I want to blame her for running into me. On top of this, it seems I'm unable to drop any argument with her until she admits that it was her fault for getting it started. I know this can't be right. But even though I'm beginning to suspect that my view of these things may be mistaken, I seem helpless to do otherwise. *Any* suggestions would be appreciated.

Answer: It's impossible to change these conditions until you begin to recognize the unconscious parts of yourself responsible for their continuation. So, with that in mind, but only if you really want to see the real cause of this conflict between you, here's a three-word solution guaranteed to change these contentious moments between the two of you. The next time you start to find something to blame, just think to yourself: "*Maybe I'm wrong.*" And then *really* consider that you might be. Deliberately taking time to see your own state of mind in these moments is the same as choosing to see that—regardless of how you want to justify it—*negativity* never *knows what's right.*

KEY LESSONS

1. Being renewed by love, and beginning your life all over again, are one and the same interior action. It starts with becoming aware of, and then bringing a conscious end to, all lingering relationships you may have with old thoughts and feelings that want you to keep seeing your life through their eyes.

2. Here's why fighting with your partner never changes *anything* real: your struggle is not with whomever seems to oppose you, but rather with what you have yet to understand about the opposing forces that live within you.

3. It's impossible for us to be truly patient and kind with our partner, to hold them in a compassion that heals, until we have learned the only right thing to do with our own pain which is … to bring it into the light of higher awareness.

10

The ABCs of Relationship Magic

I'm sure that teaching techniques have changed over these many years since I was a child, but also that the basic fundamentals of what we had to learn "back in the day" remain the same. So, assuming that things haven't changed that much, all of us still have to learn basic math tables, writing skills, and of course the alphabet.

In much the same way, there are a few basic principles we need to know if our wish is to learn how to nourish a loving relationship between our partner and ourself. We can call these basic tenets the ABCs of relationship magic. However—and it must be stressed at this point—the world in which most of us grew up knew little to nothing of these essential codes—requirements, really—for love to grow beyond the limitations inherent in the unconscious demands that we tend to place on our partner. These same indispensable fundamentals are little known, let alone adhered to today.

Rather, and to the point of these first few comments, we learned much of what we did about love and relationships—the good, the bad, and the ugly—by watching "adults" interact. Not just the behavior of our own parents, and how they treated (or mistreated) one another, but we were also influenced by the depiction of these relationships as we watched them being acted out on TV, or in popular movies.

With very few other examples to model our own relationships after, we learned to imitate certain commonly seen behaviors; in this instance, we adopted—as our own—three fundamental, but ultimately imperfect, ways of dealing with our partner...especially when we think they've "done us wrong" one way or another.

At this point, if I were speaking before a group of students, I would tell them, "Take a deep breath." As a teacher, this is my way of indicating that what I'm about to say next is likely going to challenge some cherished beliefs, or cultivated image. Therefore, do your best not to get stressed; remain as open as possible.

So...my dear reader, take a deep breath.

I trust you will see the insights about to be offered for what they are: *loving friends of anyone* who wishes to realize, and then outgrow, a body of unseen love-limiting beliefs that are keeping you and your partner from unconditionally loving one another. There is no judgment in what follows, but this I must leave for you to see.

We live—at least for now, and for the majority of those I know—from a nature that believes getting angry with the one we love is a natural and necessary act; as if lashing out verbally (heaven forbid, physically) at our partner is something we've no other choice but to do any time our partner "pushes" us to that breaking point.

We also believe, accordingly, that making up after a fight is how we reset the relationship. Some of the ways we try to straighten out these messy moments is by having "make-up sex," offering profuse apologies, buying each other gifts, or taking "start over" trips so that we never do "that" again. We see such acts as being the solution to the suffering we either induced or that we felt we had to endure "for the sake of love."

Second on this list of false beliefs—again, pretty much standard issue—is the idea that blaming our partner for how we feel, i.e., letting them know they've been judged and found guilty, is in both of our best interests.

On one hand, we're relieved—for the moment, any-way—from our pain by dumping it on them, making certain they can see what we feel they've done against us. At the same time, *they're* given fair warning to straighten out their act, or to face the consequences. In our mind, the very least they should do is thank us for telling them what they need to do to make things right between us again!

The last of these false actions is to try and coerce our partner to change. In other words, when the first two methods prove futile, fail as they must, then it's time to turn to the last resort: some form of *intimidation*.

Let's be clear here: we don't actually think to ourselves, at least I hope not, "Let me find some way to make my partner bend to my will." But when we start with the "cold shoulder" routine, threatening to walk out, or whatever our action is to punish our partner until they acquiesce, the meaning is clear: "change or else!"

Now perhaps I'm going out on a limb here, but I don't think so. Most of us know that none of these three methods—anger, blame, and coercion—is good for anyone involved; not one of them is helpful or healing. Rather, all three are hurtful, and actually make things worse between our partner and us!

If you're following me, and agree with my assessment of the "mess" these outwardly expressed negative states make of things, then we find ourselves in a bit of a tough spot.

We want our partner to change, as we can be fairly sure is true of their wish for us. We *need* them to become more kind, considerate, patient, or compassionate in order for us to grow in the love that we share between us.

Yet, on the other hand, we also know that we can't force this kind of transformation in them, any more than we would use force to open a rosebud so that we might enjoy the beauty of its bloom.

Our situation is a little bit like getting a flat tire on some abandoned country road…and finding ourselves with no tools to make the repair. In other words, we want to help our partner change and fulfill not just their promise, but also our hope that—together—our relationship can be stronger than any weakness in our individual parts. There's only one way to make this wish come true.

If—as we have seen—we have been powerless to bring about conditions conducive to helping our partner change their ways, then it's time to take another path. Not only is it the only one left, but it's also the only one that can work:

We have to help them see the wisdom *of changing their nature, the necessity of it, so that it becomes something they're willing to do.* But it can't be *our* wisdom that motivates them, because we know how we tend to react anytime someone suggests they may know what's best for us; suffice it to say we don't exactly welcome that kind of advice.

So then, what's our role if our wish is to help our partner become conscious of whatever may be limiting them, and our partnership as well? Here's the answer:

We must give our partner the room they need to see what we know they can't yet see in themselves. The following chapter section should make it very clear why—if we love our partner, and want our love to grow—we must agree to create this special kind of healing space.

Stop Pushing Your Partner Into This Dark Shell

The first of the three letters in the ABCs of relationship magic that we're going to study is the letter "A." It stands for *anger*. Anger *is a blinding force*. Let's see why this is true.

Anytime we become angry and express our dissatisfaction because something in our partner's nature rubs us the wrong way, what happens? They become equally upset with us. The more they push back, the more they "prove" to us that we were right in our original judgment of them: there's a flaw in their character, and it's our responsibility to "fix" it. As our insistence mounts, so does their resistance to considering anything we might ask them to see about themselves. As a result, instead of helping our partner to open their eyes, our anger induces a kind of psychological blindness in them ... producing the very opposite of what we had set out to do!

We can't *make* our partner see what we see in them. We can't make our partner *feel* the way we do when, in this blindness, they treat us with inconsideration or unkindness. But the fact that now *we* can see these truths—not just about our partner's limitations, but the unseen role we've played in their continuation—*changes everything*.

We've seen that any anger we express toward our partner pushes them into a kind of psychological shell from within which they see nothing other than someone hurting them—an adversary they must attack, or from whom they must escape. We shouldn't have to imagine this kind of blindness. We've all been pushed into that same painful corner many times where we said and did things that we later regret.

But now that our eyes are open, we see what we couldn't before. *It's impossible to point out—in anger— some limitation that we want our partner to see in their nature without blinding them to its existence at the same time!*

This last insight points to a way out of this unseen double bind that we've been caught in with the one we love. It also tells us that *before* we can help our partner see, and then want to change, some troubling feature in their nature, we too must make a change.

When the one we love "steps on our toes"—says, or does, something to make us mad—we must agree to replace our resistance toward our partner with the following realization, and then act on it as follows: The only chance our partner has to see their limitation is if we will agree to *give up the anger that we feel toward them for not being who and what we demand they ought to be.*

I can almost hear what I know many of my readers are thinking right about now. It goes something like this: "Oh yeah…right; sure, just stop getting mad! As if I haven't tried to do that already. I mean…really; exactly how am I supposed get over this kind of anger?"

To be completely honest with you, it took me several days of writing to complete the next short section of this chapter. And that's because there are no easy "three simple steps" or "positive affirmations" to free us from the kind of disappointment or resentment we feel whenever our partner seems to act against us or our mutual interests.

In truth, nothing can prepare us for those moments when the only way to help our partner rise above one of their limitations is by agreeing to see our own in that same moment. And in case there's any doubt about this, all negative reactions are limitations.

What this means, as best I can explain it, is that learning "how" to give up this kind of negativity can't be separated from the moment "when" it appears. Let me explain this unusual idea:

Much as we learned "how" to swim "when" we got tossed into the water, or how we need to bend our knees when doing some heavy lifting, so we learn to give up this anger when—and as—we see the impossibility of helping our partner outgrow a limitation while trying to punish them for it at the same time.

Getting negative over seeing a fault or a weakness in our partner is not their limitation: it's ours.

If you need to, please reread and ponder this last insight until it reveals its wisdom to you. Here's what it's intended to convey:

Impatience is our limitation; this kind of irritation with our partner is like blaming them for our aching feet after we tied our own shoelaces too tight!

The same holds true with our inability to forgive, or to just let go of some petty argument or gripe.

We may not have thought of these character traits as a weakness, but what else can we call any negative reaction that finds a "good reason" to grind our partner down whenever they disappoint us in even the smallest of small ways?

Certainly it's not our partner's fault that our love for them can turn from beautiful to bitter in less time than it takes to blame them for our own pain.

Why It's Pointless to Blame
Your Partner for Your Pain

The second of the three letters in the ABCs of relationship magic is the letter "B." It stands for *blame*, and here's how it works hand in hand with the blinding effect of anger: *One of the ways that our own limitations remain hidden from us is by blaming our partner for making us aware of them.* This idea may seem confusing at first, but only until we can look at it through the eyes of our own past experience.

How many times has someone we love pointed out—especially in the heat of a moment that catches us "off guard"—some not-so-pleasant feature about us?

What's our immediate reaction to our partner pointing out a fault, a weakness, whatever you want to call it—that they can see, but that we can't? Do we say, "Oh, thank you so much for showing me that negative part of myself?"

Or is our first reaction to feel attacked, and then to defend ourselves? In a heartbeat we're on the side of something in our nature that's fighting to remain concealed, when we know that our only hope of transcending it is to see it for what it is: a limitation.

Remember our earlier lessons: nothing can be healed in us that remains concealed, and our partner serves as a "secret" agent of just such revelations! We can't refresh this last idea enough times: we are the "other" half of every pleasurable or painful experience that we have with our partner.

We are the "other" half of the joy we share, as well as one half of the suffering between our partner and ourself whenever we're together.

Can you start to see the extraordinary secret being told here, and how its wisdom, once embraced, is the same as the strength you need to drop the blame game once and for all?

For starters, blaming our partner for whatever pain we're in changes nothing, because *nothing we can blame in them has the power to change us.*

But even more importantly—keeping the above in mind—imagine for a moment the following scenario, and then do your level best—based on our discoveries together—to make the following a reality: something your partner says or does—"again"—sets you off, and up comes that usual anger, followed by the equally familiar urge to blame them for your pain.

But now you understand that your partner isn't the only one involved in the appearance of this pain; rather, they have just helped you to see the limited parts of yourself that *always* react in the same negative way, over the same unwanted thing!

Yes, it's a shock; every revelation that precedes the healing it allows for does just that. So you take a deep breath, and allow your realization to choose a new action for you, one that you never before thought possible:

Instead of blaming your partner for making you aware of some limitation in yourself, you say—silently to yourself—*"Thank you. I didn't know that about myself."* With that, the miracle begins: as your usual resistance to whatever they've revealed in you disappears, so does their insistence that you change *because you're doing it...on the spot!* Now instead of reliving old resentments, a new kind of love grows between you. Effortless respect for one another replaces your demand for it.

Any Use of Force to Change
Your Partner Is an Exercise in Futility

Before we move on to study the next, and last, letter in the ABCs of relationship magic, let's make sure that we haven't created any mistaken ideas that may cloud the central lesson of this last chapter section.

We are *not* saying that we shouldn't feel pain over what our partner may have done in some unthinking moment.

Nor are we saying that our partner is somehow excused for mistreating us, or that they aren't without responsibility to make proper amends, as the moment calls for. In truth, pretending that we haven't been hurt by a loved one is a kind of poison; it kills the possibility of our work together to reveal, heal, and transcend whatever remains incomplete within us, and between us, accordingly.

The point is that getting angry, blaming our partner for our pain, does nothing but blind both of us to the real reason we're together in the first place: to help each other see—and then step past—the parts of ourselves that stand in the way of our sharing higher and higher levels of love. Now, keeping this idea in mind, let's look at the third, and last, of the three letters in the ABCs of relationship magic. The letter "C" stands for *coercion.*

When we look up the word "coercion" in the dictionary, here's what we find: "*to compel by force, intimidation, or authority, especially without regard for individual desire or volition.*"[10] Sounds a little extreme, doesn't it? Perhaps not!

We may have never seen it in this way, but what else is the "silent treatment," the "cold shoulder," or that swift look of disapproval that we give our partner if not an at-

---

10. "Coercion," Dictionary.com (accessed 2018).

tempt to get them back in line, marching to the beat of our drum?

We don't need an interpreter to read these wordless actions. We know their meaning: something about you is getting under my skin, so knock it off. Now! And, of course, should our partner fail to heed these early warning signs, then, at some point, we know what comes next. We reach the "last straw." One way or another, we voice some form of overt threat whose meaning can't be missed: "Either get busy and change, or *face the consequences!*" These are desperate times. After all, what other choice have we?

To date—by and large, anyway—nothing we've said or done to our partner has caused them to have a change of heart. To us it's clear that they can't possibly love us, at least not as we love them, or they would have already complied with our earlier, less emphatic request they change their ways. All told, we see their refusal to deal with what we told them disturbs us as a rejection of our love. But it is not. *We've mistaken inability for unwillingness.* Until we can see and understand this important distinction, nothing real can change—in them, or between us.

It's not that our partner doesn't want to outgrow their limitations. Even a moment's consideration proves that just can't be true; no one would ever consciously agree to be less than his or her possibilities allow. So, *what we see as our partner's stubborn refusal to acknowledge a fault is actually their unawareness of it*. Let's pause here for a moment and take a closer look at what's causing this misperception, as well as all of the pain that comes with it.

FIRST

We have a widely held, but false, belief that pointing out some fault in our partner's character is the same as their being able to see that imperfection at the same time! Again, we are mistaken. How can we be sure? An honest answer to the following question gives us all the proof we need: Do *we* see the fault in ourself when our partner tries to point it out, or do we see our partner at fault for picking on us, or worse, doubting our perfection?

SECOND

So much of the compulsion that drives the demands we make on our partner to change is rooted in our unseen insistence that they should be as free of their limitations *as we imagine ourselves to be free of our own*.

This insistence—that they see the "mote in their eye"—distracts us from seeing the "beam" in our own, so that not only are we trying to force our partner to see a fault in their character that they've yet to realize on their own, but we're suffering from a similar kind of blindness. We can't see that we're little to nothing like what we're demanding our partner to be: patient, compassionate, and lovingly kind.

Here's a brief summary of this last important lesson: we can't force our partner to see whatever may be their present limitations; we can only free them to do so. Which brings us to the last section of this chapter and the book.

A Pair of Special Exercises to Help You and Your Partner Grow Together

If we want to help our partner to change, *we* must change. There is no other way. And more: unless we're exceptionally blessed, it's unlikely our partner has the same wish that we do: to keep growing and exploring a love that, at the start, was filled with surprising changes, but that has lost some of that sparkle because one or both of us has stopped changing.

All this is to say: odds are, you're the one who will have to initiate the work needed to refresh your relationship. No problem. You'll find everything you need to get started in the two special relationship exercises that follow. They are designed to work in a two-fold way.

Part one unfolds as you initiate the first action and receive the revelation that will help make changes in you. The second part of the exercise happens as your partner sees and experiences this change in you. When you no longer act toward them in the old way, they can't help but see their own mechanical nature that only knows the "old way" to react to you.

In effect, your new actions help to reveal their old limitations so that—for a moment, anyway—and to whatever degree it occurs, your partner suddenly sees the need to change! If ever there was a real "win-win" situation, a way for two people to realize the highest possibilities a relationship can offer, this is it.

Exercise #1: Look Within Yourself
Before You "Speak Out"

Let's say you're with your partner and you see something in their character that "strikes a familiar nerve" in you. Maybe it's impatience, an obvious pretense, or just the unpleasant tone in their voice when they say something unkind or otherwise painful to your ear. There are so many options here, but suffice it to say that it's whatever "stone" they seem to put in your shoe in that moment.

You suddenly feel a negative reaction start to course through you, generally attended by an unspoken thought along the lines of *"there they go again."* As a rule, the next thing that happens is you feel obligated to give this negative feeling a voice. After all, if you don't point out their misstep how will they know they've stepped out of line, let alone how they've troubled you?

But now thanks to your studies, you understand that whatever you feel compelled to point out to your partner causes them to immediately oppose you, pushing your observation away at the same time. So that now—rather than taking your habitual place in this old pattern—you meet the moment with your new intention: *you look within yourself* before *you "speak out."* And what do you see?

Call it what you will—however you want to describe it—there stands revealed some kind of pain; perhaps anger, an old resentment, a sense of disappointment. By whatever name, *it's* negative. *But you're not...* and here's why: your new awareness of this unconscious nature is the same as your freedom from its compulsion to prove itself right.

Your conscious struggle to bear its pressure in you—to not let it push you to speak *its* pain—is the same as sparing your partner the brunt of its dark nature.

You are changed on the spot because now—thanks to the exercise of looking within before you speak out—you can see, clearly, who you can no longer agree to be.

In the meantime, actually at the same time of your revelations, your partner is watching you. It may not seem so, but in the same moment of their misstep they could feel your negative reaction. Even if you think you masked it for fear of an unwanted encounter, your partner feels that dark energy. It unconsciously registers within them, creating an opposing reaction. So your partner is waiting, albeit unaware that they're preparing to defend themselves from what they think you're about to say!

But not a contrary word slips out of your mouth. You're busy learning about yourself, *and your silence is deafening to them.* It's giving your partner the momentary room—and the freedom—they need to see that the only thing punishing them at the moment is their own defensive thoughts and feelings. They're ready to fight... but your silence has left them no one to fight with! They're left alone with their pain, with no one they can blame for its mounting pressure. This new awareness is the same as their realization of a limitation in their nature they would have never seen otherwise. What was concealed is revealed, and the healing can begin because now your partner has seen the need to change.

Exercise #2: Drop Your End of This Unseen Tug-of-War

All forms of competition between partners breed conflict, especially in the unconscious form that it takes in what seems—on the surface—to be a casual conversation.

It all starts as simply as you wanting to tell your partner about something that you did that day; perhaps to share an insight you gained, or just to talk through some condition at work or at home that's concerning you.

No more do you finish your sentence—or are right in the middle of your words—than your partner interrupts you. They've decided to change the topic—on the spot—to one that's obviously more interesting than whatever it was you had to say. They start talking about themselves!

Now maybe you show it, maybe you don't, but you're hurt. So you do one of two things: you either pull the conversation back in the direction you intended it to go, or you sit there, tune out your partner, and have a dialogue with yourself about how all your partner can do is think about themselves.

Of course, you could tell your partner about how self-centered they are by always hogging the spotlight but, as a rule, they'll just take your comments as proof that you want the stage all to yourself. If you want things to change, to end this unseen tug-of-war between the two of you, then try the following exercise.

The next time you begin to talk about yourself to your partner and they step in front of you—in order to talk about themselves—don't compete for the stage. Let them have the center spotlight.

Don't compete with them. Allow them the room they need to complete feeding the unconscious parts of themselves that believe they're the only thing that matters in this world.

Don't contest their solo performance. And, to the best of your ability, don't judge it either. Instead, witness it and yourself at the same time. You'll see that most of the pain you feel in these moments isn't because your partner wants to steal the show, but rather because you want the same thing that they do: some attention.

We all want to be the main attraction, and some seem to need it more than others. The more clearly you see this, the less interest you'll have in the parts of yourself that always want to fight for that part.

On the other side of this equation, by giving your partner the stage all to themselves, you help make it possible for them to see how empty it is to be on it all alone. They may not change their "act" all at once; in fact, it's unlikely. But, for your choice to no longer compete for the "top spot," you're awarded the "Freedom" prize for best supporting actor.

Let Love Be Your Answer

Perhaps you've read the classic novel *The Count of Monte Cristo* by Alexandre Dumas, or hopefully you've had a chance to see one of the film versions made over the last fifty years or so.

Very briefly, it's a powerful story that unfolds in an early nineteenth-century coastal city in France, where love takes its three central characters on a long journey of revelation, and the eventual realization of what matters most in their lives.

The hero, Edmond Dantès, is accused of a murder that he didn't commit, by Fernand, a lifelong friend, who is the one who actually committed the crime. Fernand is so jealous that Edmond has the love of Mercédès, the heroine, that he ensures Edmond is thrown into a hellacious, inescapable prison, and left there to die. But when, after many torturous years in captivity, Edmond manages to escape by a series of almost impossible coincidences, he plots an elaborate scheme of revenge against those who betrayed him.

As the story nears its climactic end, Mercédès, whom Edmond never stopped loving—and who never stopped loving him—sees through his elaborate charade (as the Count of Monte Cristo), and learns of his plan to take revenge on Fernand.

She begs him to let go of his anger, to give up the fight raging in his heart, and to forgo hatred in favor of remembering the love they shared before fate tore them apart. At this point, and the reason for this brief summary, he makes the unbelievably honest and brutal response that I'll paraphrase here:

"Please, I beg you, don't take from me the only thing I have left: my hatred."

He goes on to plead that she leave him alone, and to let him exact the revenge he has planned. He explains it's the only way he knows to win back a life that was stolen from him.

We don't need to learn much more about this one scene, since it's the turning point in the story. In the end, she helps him remember, *to feel*, what really matters the most. He lets go. They fall into each other's arms. Love wins the day.

In this story, Edmond and Fernand—the two leading male characters—play opposing roles: one who is betrayed by his friend, and the other the friend who betrays him in order to win the love of Mercédès, whom, he finds out too late, he will never possess.

Mercédès, the female lead, represents higher wisdom. She understands there is no winning side to any fight when the cost of that struggle is to lose sight of what matters most in life: love.

I've taken the time to summarize this part of the love story because we can look into this relationship between Edmond and Mercédès and use it much as we might a mirror. Within it we will see not only certain distinct similarities between our partner and ourself, but also—if we look closely enough—some wonderful new possibilities for us, as well.

Have you ever been drawn into a fight with a loved one where—by the time you got knee-deep into who's "right" and who's "wrong," maybe over the most trivial of matters—it felt as if, somehow, your very life depended on the outcome of that fight?

We've all had moments like this, perhaps too many times; which is why it seems strange that we've yet to see the following: there's no such thing as a "winning" side in any fight between two people who love one another, any more than one seat proved itself better than another on the deck of the Titanic.

This isn't to say that there aren't, and won't always be, differences in opinion between our partner and us; this is natural; needed, actually. There will always be some differences between us that aren't a question of which of us is right—or wrong, as the case may be; rather, there may come times when a disagreement might be over the best course to take for the well-being of a child, or over some other shared concern...where we see a different path than does our partner in order to reach an outcome that both of us agree is for the good of all. So, to that end, let us agree that there's a *big* distinction between working through our differences—creating together a choice that's palatable to both of us—versus trying to shove what we believe is right down the throat of our partner.

Our demands never prove we're right, any more than our negativity proves our partner is wrong. The only thing this kind of stress and strain between us proves is that *we're missing at least one piece of the puzzle* in that struggle with our partner.

Again, what's the missing piece? We can call it "love." But if the word—or even the ideal—had the power to hold us together when everything feels like it's trying to pull us apart—especially in the throes of a fight—then all we would have to do is call up that word, and our world would suddenly be right.

To be clear: love is not just a word; *it's an action.* It's a choice we agree to make when we see—by the light of a higher order of understanding—that there's something more important at stake in that moment than struggling to satisfy our own self-centered interests.

In this instance, one such new action would be to use the onset of any conflict, regardless of who initiates it...to fight for something higher than who will be the next "king of the hill." In other words, rather than fighting with your partner, fight instead *to remember how destructive it is to your love to tear into one another*... over anything.

Let me anticipate what you may be feeling at this point, and answer that fear: Don't fight to "get on top" of any thought that tries to tell you, warn you, "But, if I don't fight back, my partner will walk all over me." Instead, fight to see how much pain there is in any compulsion—whether your partner's, or your own—to have the last word. Then you won't want to win that kind of power for yourself, and neither will you want to punish your partner for the same.

If we will dare to interrupt the usual pattern of fighting with our partner—pause just long enough to even consider this new action—we will see in that same moment what love has been wanting to show us all along: any argument with our partner—where one of us is trying to prove we're right, and the other wrong —is *not* because we know "better," and it's certainly *not* born of love. In these moments, we fight for one reason, and for one reason only no matter how you want to call it: *love is absent.*

In a way, this is all we need to know, all we need to see, because when that telling moment comes we won't be tempted to start looking for yet another false solution. If we see, no matter how dimly, that love is the only answer, then we know our new response must be to refuse to fight.

On another note: yes, it's likely that your partner won't understand what you're trying to do, and may still want to fight. But, eventually, they'll see how useless it is to pick a fight when they can't find the "old you" to fight with. Each time you choose to leave them there with their enmity, but with no "enemy" to legitimize it, they'll have little choice but to let it go, whatever "it" is in that moment. This may take a while, but you'll soon see the birth of an altogether new relationship between the two of you.

Practicing Love Makes Perfect Love

A brilliant, but still very young, musical genius goes to see her teacher, a master pianist with whom she is in training. Knowing her own tendency to get so tense while she performs that she'll strike the wrong keys, she's frightened about an important upcoming recital, and has come to seek his guidance, if not his blessings.

"I'm trying, I really am," she says, "but I just don't seem to be making any real progress when it comes time to perform." And pausing there to take in a deep breath, followed by a sigh just loud enough for the master to hear it—so as to win some sympathy from him—she finishes her thought:

"I want…to be like you; I want to…play, flawlessly, in front of an audience just like I watch you do."

She looks up at him, briefly, to see if he's reacting at all. But if he is, his eyes don't show it, and for some reason this makes her rush to get on with the rest of her thoughts.

"When I'm by myself, or playing for my friend, I have no problems. There are no glitches, missed notes, every movement seems to come out perfect. But the minute it really counts, the moment it's time to shine before an audience, it feels like all that I've worked so hard to learn... I don't know; like it just leaves me as if I never practiced the piece at all."

The teacher looks at her and slightly raises his eyebrows, indicating that he knows she has more to say. She receives his invitation, and goes on to ask him the question she has come there to ask.

"Please help me, master, what am I supposed to do? How will I ever get to the point where I can play as well for others as I do when I practice by myself?"

A smile crosses his face, putting her at ease. Then he says, "Many years ago, I went to my teacher asking him pretty much this same question that you've brought to me. Would you like to hear what he told me? Because what I learned back then—the answer that he gave to me—is the same as I would give to you now... if that's your wish."

"Yes, please," she says, "I'd really like that."

"My master said that 'without practice there is no perfection, but the real perfection of any piece must include its repeated performance under the most difficult circumstances.'"

He pauses for a moment to ask: "You do understand that much, don't you?"

She answers in the affirmative, adding an afterthought she doesn't really mean to speak. "But, why…does it have to be that way?"

"Because only then—and there, in moments that no practice can prepare you for—are you shown your present limitations."

The teacher smiles at her again, in part because he wants to encourage her; but he is also remembering, with gratitude, how his journey to being a respected master began the day his own teacher asked him the same question he is about to ask his own student.

"Can you see we would never be able to see our imperfections—whatever our level of performance—if there wasn't something *already* perfect within us?"

By the look that comes over her face, he realizes she isn't quite following. So, after taking a moment to think through a way to make his point clearer, he adds another thought.

"Think of it this way: just as we would never see our own shadow if it weren't for the light of the sun revealing it to us, neither would we ever be able to see our own limitations without something—call that presence what you

will—showing them to us. The light of this higher awareness lets us see that not only are there endless levels to this
music that waits to be more perfectly performed, but that
for our insight gained by this same awareness...we're the
one invited to play it!"

"Yes," she says, "although I never quite saw it that way."

"Then let's look deeper. How else can you explain
your feeling that there's much more to a passage you just
played than you were able to express as you played it...if
not for the fact that, in some way, *it* tells you so?"

"Yes," she says again, and this time with more enthusi-
asm. "Yes, of course. If I understand you correctly, you're
saying that even though we have a definite role in its realization, we are not the ones who perfect the music we play.
Rather, it perfects us so that we might be able to express it
ever more perfectly."

"That's the deal; try not to forget it. We don't practice
to *prove* ourselves competent. As you've already seen—and
are hopefully learning—that approach breeds fear, and a
growing sense of doubt. We practice in order to discover—
to be shown at once—our limitations *and our limitless
ability to transcend them*. By striving to be as true as we
can to this understanding, and embracing the revelations
it brings, the rest is done for us."

So it is with love.

Choose to Love and Let Love
Set You and Your Partner Free

We don't perfect love; but, if we're willing—if we will choose to practice love in any one of the many ways we've looked at throughout this book—then, in exchange, it will help to perfect the love between our partner and us. In exchange for this special kind of labor that love asks us to undertake, it gives us, at once, two immeasurable gifts in return:

First comes the gift of being shown the self-limiting parts of ourself that are keeping us from realizing the unconditional love we wish to share with our partner.

For our willingness to embrace these healing revelations—*without resisting their appearance*—comes love's second and greatest gift, as follows: in that same light by which love shows us where we now love imperfectly, not only do we see the possibility of transcending that limited level of self, but we are also empowered—in that same moment—to give it up...if we so choose. And *choose* is the operative word here.

Higher love, the kind of unconditional patience and tenderness that heals old wounds, that helps us to be compassionate, kind, encouraging, and forbearing of our partner's limitations, is a choice we must make not just every day, but in every moment with everyone we know. It's a practice we must choose or we will lose its priceless gift.

So, before we close this last section of the book, let's revisit twelve of the most important lessons—a few from each chapter—that we've studied throughout our journey together. At first glance, they may seem to be quite different, but through all of them runs a single golden thread, as follows:

Each one is a secret invitation to practice love. All of them suggest a completely new way to look at unwanted moments with your partner by laying down "your side" of that problem long enough to see not just the "other" side, but that no one side of any suffering between you tells the whole story.

Taken all together they point to the possibility that we are all on an endless journey, being perfectly guided by love to realize a perfect partnership...not just with the one we love, but with Love itself that wants only to perfect us.

1. The real problem we have with others is what we don't yet see and understand about ourselves.

2. Our relationships help reveal what's concealed in us that needs to be healed.

3. Once we learn what it means to "see ourselves"—to accept each such revelation as a herald of the healing that it brings—then we will not only understand what it means to accept "others" as they are...but we will also learn to be quietly grateful for what

they have come to teach us about ourselves, as they pass through our life.

4. Seeing ourselves *as we are* allows us to see what our partner is looking at, at the same time!

5. It's not by ignoring the differences between our partner and ourself that we get past how they "rub" us wrong; but rather by learning to use them—as does the jeweler his polishing wheel—to help perfect both of us, not only as lovers and friends, but also as individuals.

6. When it comes to being partners with the one we love...any time we fight, each of us is responsible for whatever may be happening to both of us.

7. Opposing forces are powerless to change their own patterns; they can only repeat themselves.

8. Despite any appearance to the contrary, it's not our partner, nor is it we, who strike the first blow in any dispute: *It's pain that picks the fight.*

9. The pain in any moment of conflict is neither just our own, nor is it just our partner's; it exists as it does because—one way or another—we're (in it) together; which means...that pain is ours.

10. We are in each other's life to help each other learn how to love one another...perfectly.

11. Our negative reactions have no awareness of themselves at all, which means that not only are they blind, but they are also incapable of loving anything.

12. If we will do our part, love will do the rest...but we must choose to put it to the test. With love, all things are possible.

Helpful Questions and Answers

Question: It feels like my partner and I have come to a dead end in our relationship. I don't think he's aware of it, but I sure am. I do love him, but...I can't let go of an old resentment that always rears its ugly head anytime he acts out one particular part of his nature that I just can't stand. I've spoken to him about this, but he just doesn't see what I'm talking about. It seems he won't change, and I can't seem to drop my resentment. How can I break these chains?

Answer: Any growing feeling of resentment toward our partner begins with closing our eyes to just how similar is our own characteristic to the one we judge in them. Here's a big hint: weakness always pounces on weakness. The end of feeling this kind of resentment comes with seeing the above as being true. In this same revelation is also the birth of compassion.

As far as your feeling of having reached the end of your road together, never forget the following: nothing in the universe has the power to stop you and your partner from starting your relationship all over; nothing, that is, except for one thing: the temptation to identify with unconscious parts of yourself that want you to believe that the limit of your present understanding about your unwanted situation is the same as the limit of your possibilities to transcend it.

Question: First, I'll admit to being a little put off by some of your ideas about what it takes to be a more loving, considerate partner; however, I also have to admit that neither have my own ideas proven much use in the "better relationships department." So, I'm trying to be open to some of what you suggest here, but there's a very doubtful voice in me saying, "What's the use? You don't have what it takes to make it to the end of this journey." I feel stuck, so any comments would be appreciated.

Answer: For one thing, it isn't *your* job to make it to the "end" of whatever you imagine is the "end" of love's possibilities, for love and its possibilities are *endless*, in every meaning of the word. So forget everything else but this: *your job is just to take the first step*, nothing more, nothing less. The rest happens naturally, as the illustration that follows makes clear.

Imagine a man trekking up a steep mountain path. All he sees ahead of him is what looks too hard for him to climb. But he takes one step at a time until—with what feels like the last step he can take—he summits a small ledge. Waiting there for him, spread out before his grateful eyes, is a view so beautiful it almost moves him to tears. He's thankful he took that last step because, otherwise, he'd have never known such a place exists for anyone who will suffer the challenge it takes to reach it. All of his doubts, even his fatigue, fall away. He looks up, and can't help himself from wanting to climb higher.

The fact that there are real places like this, not just on some distant mountain, but also waiting for you in the depths of your heart, is why your lower nature speaks to you in disparaging tones; it wants to discourage you from embarking on your journey to know higher love. It senses, in some strange way, that even the smallest step you take in this upward direction is the same *as walking away from its influence over you, and your relationship with the one you love.* So, take that step, no matter how small, shaky, or uncertain. Take it. Let love prove to you that whatever it asks of you—no matter how impossible it may seem at the moment—it will provide you in your time of need.

KEY LESSONS

1. Our task with those we love is not to push them to the end of what we imagine will mark the fulfillment of their possibilities. Any form of coercion we call on to achieve that kind of goal guarantees that neither we, nor our partner, will *ever* reach it. If we

want our partner to change, we must be willing to walk with them into—and through—any moment of limitation until *both* of us see the need to let go of it, and to make a new beginning.

2. Studying higher ideas about love without doing the work it takes to put them into practice is like gathering kernels of wheat, laying them in a row on some back shelf in your cupboard, and hoping they will produce an abundant harvest right where they sit.

3. Pain, regardless of where or how it appears in our relationship, can remain—as has been the case—the seed of a distress between us destined to flower into a mounting resentment. Or we can choose to use this same pain consciously, transforming it into the seed of something altogether new, true, and beautiful: the birth of a new level of self-understanding—the realization of a higher order of love in us, and between us—that can never turn against itself or anyone else.

Love is the magic that transforms all things into power and beauty. It brings plenty out of poverty, power out of weakness, loveliness out of deformity, sweetness out of bitterness, light out of darkness, and produces all blissful conditions out of its own substantial but indefinable essence.

~James Allen [11]

---

11. *The Spiritual Writings of James Allen* (Germany: Jazzybee Verlag, 2014).

A Few Last Words
of Encouragement

Clearly, some experiences are far more impactful than others. The truth is that most moments in our life simply flow right by us, unnoticed; almost as if we're sitting by a great river, and only made aware of its seamless waters when something being carried along by them catches our eye.

The following short story recounts one such experience that did more than catch my eye; it helped change the way I now look at every relationship in my life, *including how I see myself*.

In other words, although this event itself has long disappeared "downstream," merging its substance into the distant past, to this day its lesson remains a fixture in my perception of friends and family alike, a kind of North Star in the constellation of my consciousness. That's why I felt certain that sharing this experience with you would prove itself the perfect way to bring a happy ending to our studies together.

As you'll see, especially if you'll embrace the power of the timeless principle that it helps illustrate, the loving patience and deep kindness you'll need to succeed with this interior work of "waking up together" will soon be shining into and through your heart, mind, and soul. Here's the true story.

It all started very innocently: I had run out to the local market to pick up just a quick handful of items; my decision that I didn't need a cart turned out to be a mistake, so that my hands and arms were full as I approached the area where one pays for their groceries. But as I drew closer to the front area of the store where a number of cashiers are ordinarily waiting to check people out, it was evident that whoever was supposed to be managing customer service…must have momentarily checked out himself! There were only three cashiers with what looked like over twenty people divided into three long checkout lines…and most with carts chock-full of groceries.

So, I did what I imagine most of us do in situations like that: as I walked forward, I took an instant survey of the length of each of the three lines, estimating the number of items in the carts of those shoppers standing there, and then walked straight to the line that I felt sure would get me out of the store with the least amount of waiting time. Oh boy, was I wrong!

All too soon it became evident that out of the three lines I could have picked, my choice proved itself the slowest of all. And, sure enough, it wasn't too long before everyone else in line with me noticed this as well. That's when it started.

Two carts ahead of me, a middle-aged man began to grumble under his breath; the words were unintelligible, but the meaning was clear. He wasn't happy with the speed at which the shoppers ahead of him were being checked out and bagged. Apparently, his negativity was contagious.

A moment later, the lady directly behind him—and just in front of me—voiced, out loud, what I imagine most everyone in that line—including me, at the moment—was feeling:

"Come on!" she said. "What gives here... I mean, really? Could this line go any slower than it is?" And then, as often happens with any mob behavior, the negativity of one person seems to give a license to everyone else, and another person in line chimed in:

"I know; can you believe it... I will *never* shop at this store again!"

As I stood there, feeling this current of negative energy coursing through several of the people in line, something made me turn my attention to the cashier. She was showing the strain of standing there—likely for several hours now—having to silently suffer the brunt of the dark remarks being cast upon her skill as a cashier.

The interesting thing is that the crowd's evident displeasure with her did not help her to speed up the work she was doing; instead, it did just the opposite. As her stress mounted, so did the number of mistakes she made, requiring her to call for a supervisor to clear the cash register. You can just imagine how that went over with the people who already wanted to "stone" her.

At any rate, by the time I reached my turn to check out, I could sense her trembling from head to toe. And even though the store was ice cold, tiny beads of sweat were starting to form on her brow. So, as my turn came, and we stood there face-to-face, it was evident that other than a cursory meeting of our eyes—to acknowledge one another—she had no interest, whatsoever, in looking at me. Who could blame her? No doubt, all she had seen in the eyes of the people checking out ahead of me was some form of hostility toward her. So, as I stood there, I called up the lightest tone I could and, with a little laugh underpinning my voice, I said, "Some days are quite the adventure, aren't they!"

Almost immediately she lifted her eyes and met mine. Visibly relieved to see that I was friend, and not foe, she took a bit of a deep breath and did her best to smile back at me. I took it as permission to finish the thought behind my opening remark.

"Never mind them," I said to her, still in that moment of our relationship. "Seems everybody is in a bit of a rush these days, and sometimes impatience can get the best of us."

She was still looking at me, trying to drink in something of the soothing energy I was hoping to convey. "Anyway," I continued, "I'm not in any real hurry, so take your time."

Then came the lesson…a special kind of "gift" I never could have imagined in a thousand years. My hope here, in fact the whole reason for writing this closing section of the book, is that by sharing it with you, you might be enriched too…and then go on to share a measure of it with all those you love.

She smiled a real smile at me, and said: "Thank you *so much* for your patience. I'm doing the best I can, but I'm a new cashier at this store and…I'm still in training."

I laughed, and said: "Well, aren't we all!"

She got it, instantly, and in that moment of our shared understanding, two complete strangers became new friends. Not only that, but as I walked out of the store, grocery bag in hand, I uttered a silent thanks to the stars above me. Something remarkable had happened: unlike the unhappy shoppers standing there, regretting their "misfortune" for having to wait in that long line…I left full of gratitude for the whole experience.

The Timeless Exercise of Waking Up Together

When it comes to loving one another, waking up together, not only are we all still learning its innumerable possibilities—going through with each other what we must in order to become more loving toward one another—but this kind of higher love has no end to the lessons it has to teach us.

In other words: when it comes to love we are all, and always will be ... *in training!*

This means we are going to make mistakes with how we treat one another; we're going to come up "short" when it comes time to being forgiving and kind. Falling down "on the job" is part of the learning curve it takes to turn our new intention to be patient with one another into the new power it takes to do so. You could almost say that getting "knocked down" is how we learn to give up parts of ourself that "lead with their chin!"

Not only are we going to find ourselves set back on our heels when we run into some of the unseen limitations in our partner, but this will happen even more so ... when we encounter similar blockages in ourselves. But now, thanks to the insights our studies in higher love have revealed, we can learn to see these unwanted moments for what they have always been in reality: "on the job" training. The more evident becomes this truth—that our relationships are the way love works to "exercise" us—the more we are inwardly strengthened by our discoveries, and gradually empowered to love one another more perfectly.

As just one example, if we know that our partner is "in training," then we are a lot less likely to blame them for falling down on the job of caring for us. So not only are we able to forgive our partner for failing to meet our expectations, but at the same time, we're also empowered *to forgive ourselves* whenever we see ourselves come up short, having missed some intended mark.

Such moments—of realizing that neither we, nor our partner, are as we've imagined ourselves to be—are shocking, at best. But let's be perfectly clear: love can no more be discouraged by what it serves to reveal in us … than can the sun be shamed into not shining!

This last idea can't be stated strongly enough: when it comes to our wish—and work—to learn how to love unconditionally, *all forms of discouragement are a lie*; they are a misbegotten creation of an unconscious level of self whose intent—as expressed by the disheartened way it wants us to feel—is to make us believe that meeting these limitations in ourselves is the same as the end of love's possibilities. Use the following example to prove to yourself why this, and any such form of discouragement, is utter nonsense!

Can you remember the first time you ever tried to run a mile, or to work out with a set of weights heavier than what you may have used before? Let me refresh your memory, as needed.

The moment you pressed your body to go beyond its present level of conditioning, it started "screaming" at you; a "sound" we all know in one way or another: lungs gasping for air, heart pounding out of our chest, weary arms aching with fatigue. But why would we deliberately take our body up to and through such a threshold, especially one that brings this kind of suffering, as it always seems to do? *It's by design*: we understand there's only one way to make ourselves physically stronger: we must pay the "price" for each new level of endurance and strength that we would make our own. That's the whole purpose of working to train our body: to rise above whatever its present limitation, in order to realize the next higher level of our potential at that point in time. And then, to do it all over again, should that be our wish.

And so it is ... when it comes to the "exercise" of waking up together.

Nothing in the universe can stop us from letting go and loving our partner unconditionally, because the higher love we seek has "gone before us" to prepare the way. But what love has prepared for us doesn't mean that *we* don't have to prepare to receive its power to perfect us, and our relationships.

We have work to do.

And right now is always the right time to get started.

Out beyond ideas of wrongdoing and right doing,
there is a field. I'll meet you there.
When the soul lies down in that grass,
the world is too full to talk about.
Ideas, language, even the phrase "each other"
doesn't make any sense.

~Rumi [12]

12. Jalal al-Din Rumi, *The Essential Rumi*, trans. Coleman Barks (New York: HarperCollins, 1996).

To Contact Guy Finley about this book, write to:

Life of Learning Foundation
P.O. Box 10 RM
Merlin, OR 97532

Or visit www.guyfinley.org/free-ebook and receive one of Guy Finley's bestselling e-books as a free gift. While you're on guyfinley.org you can sign up for Guy's weekly Key Lesson E-mail Newsletter, delivered once a week right to your desktop. You can also enjoy free MP3 downloads and videos, read volumes of published and unpublished works, browse the bookstore, and have free access to a host of other invaluable resources, including frequently asked questions, archived Key Lessons, and free podcasts.

Follow Guy Finley on Facebook (www.guyfinley.org/facebook), Twitter (www.guyfinley.org/twitter), and YouTube (www.guyfinley.org/youtube).

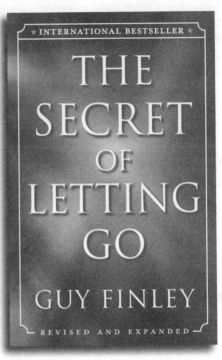

★ INTERNATIONAL BESTSELLER ★

THE
SECRET
OF
LETTING
GO

GUY FINLEY

REVISED AND EXPANDED

The Secret of Letting Go
Guy Finley

Llewellyn is proud to present the revised and expanded edition of our bestselling self-help book, *The Secret of Letting Go* by Guy Finley. Featuring an attractive new cover and fresh material, this Finley classic has been updated inside and out.

With more than two millions copies of all of his books in print, Guy Finley's message of self-liberation has touched people around the world. Discover how to extinguish self-defeating thoughts and habits that undermine true happiness. Exploring relationships, depression, and stress, his inspiring words can help you let go of debilitating anxiety, unnecessary anger, paralyzing guilt, and painful heartache. True stories, revealing dialogues, and thought-provoking questions will guide you toward the endless source of inner strength and emotional freedom that resides within us all.

978-0-7387-1198-0, 312 pp., 5 ³/₁₆ x8   **$15.99**

NOTES

NOTES

NOTES

_____

_____

_____

_____

_____

_____

_____

_____

_____

_____

_____

_____

_____

_____

_____

_____

_____

_____

_____

NOTES